Remembering
Tony Jarvis

Portrait of a Headmaster

Richard Hawley

ISBN: 978-1-7923-7649-8
Library of Congress Control Number: 2021919728

Printed in the United States of America

Publisher: Short Story America
Design: Soundview Design

Requests for such permissions should be addressed to:

Short Story America
1276 Harbour Town Drive
Orange Park, FL 32065
Visit us online at www.shortstoryamerica.com

Also by Richard Hawley

FICTION
The Three Lives of Jonathan Force
Greeves Passing
The Source of Longing
The Other World
The Guru
Paul and Julianna
The Headmaster's Papers
The Headmaster's Wife

POETRY
Twenty-One Visits with a Darkly Sun-Tanned Angel
The Headmaster's Poems
St. Julian
With Love to My Survivors
Aspects of Vision

NON-FICTION
Forward and No Retreat: Two Centuries of Linsly School Life
I Can Learn from You: Boys as Relational Learners (with Michael Reichart)
Souls in Boxes
For Whom the Boy Toils
Reaching Boys / Teaching Boys (with Michael Reichert)
Beyond the Icarus Factor
Hard Lessons and Other Talks to the School
Papers from the Headmaster
Hail University! A Century of University School Life
Mr. Chips Redux / Miss Dove Redivivus
Seeing Things: A Chronicle of Surprises
Building Drug Free Schools
The Purposes of Pleasure
A School Answers Book
Coming Through School (editor) Boys Will Be Men
Kiski: The Story of a Boys School
On My Way Out: a Reflection on Closure, Vols I, II, and III

Sir Thomas More:
Why not be a teacher? You'd be a fine teacher;
perhaps a great one.

Richard Rich:
If I was, who would know it?

More:
You; your pupils; your friends; God.
Not a bad public, that.

—Robert Bolt, *A Man for all Seasons*

CONTENTS

———————

LAST MEAL

———————

Tony's phone call was straightforward.

In prior conversations he said he was having a hard time seeing the benefit of his bi-monthly chemotherapy treatments. There were days of nausea and fatigue before he felt well enough to be about his business, and his business remained considerable, including weekly duties as associate rector of All Saints, Ashmont, his parish of forty years, commitments to baptize children of his former and far-flung students or to preside over their marriages. He did not miss the ordination of any of his students who were becoming priests. There were also final proofs to be revised and edited for his book, *Men of Roxbury,* short lives of distinguished graduates of The Roxbury Latin School over the course of its nearly four centuries of continuous operation. On any given week, he received dozens of invitations from people who wanted to meet him for a meal or just to pop by.

He had just conferred with his oncologist, and because the chemo medicines were no longer slowing the growth of the tumors in his lungs and elsewhere in his system, he decided to stop further treatment. He said his doctor told him he might have "two good months."

He called to tell me this, I think, because we have been close friends for more than half a century, and he preferred delivering what he knew would be sad news to me while he was still coherent, still himself. There were more big questions than I could possibly express, but I managed to ask him how he was feeling right now. He said he felt surprisingly good, though he tired easily. Over the phone, he sounded strong—normal. He sounded as he had always sounded.

Listening to his voice, I was put in mind of a summer evening three years ago when, in the course of what had begun as a leisurely dinner on an outdoor terrace of an upscale restaurant a short walk from his apartment in Dorchester, Tony told me that he had been diagnosed with stage four lung cancer, a terminal diagnosis. I could not make what he was saying cohere. Sitting directly across from me in the declining light, Tony looked in robust good health—good color, good energy, fit and trim. Then too the first thing I could think to ask was how are you feeling right now. He laughed. He said he felt fine, as well as he ever had. *Lung cancer?* I asked. Tony not only did not smoke, he had never smoked a single cigarette. I asked him if there was any pain, any trouble breathing. He said no, nothing.

He learned of the cancer in his lungs after a scan was taken to see if he remained cancer free after his treatment for colon cancer three years earlier, treatment of which had required surgeries and subsequent radiation and medication. Weakened and hobbled for weeks, Tony managed to carry on with his teaching duties at Yale's Divinity School, where he was directing a new program for students who were seeking vocations as teachers and school chaplains. The colon cancer had been a terrible siege, though Tony assured his friends and colleagues that he would be fine and that he was receiving the best possible medical care. He told us these things to mute our concerns which, had we expressed them at the time, would probably have amplified his own. After he recovered, I asked him what was the worst of it and at any point did he think he might die. He said that during the worst of it he would gladly have died. After his first surgery he recalled agonizing waves of pain as he lay in his own blood and excrement, helpless on the floor of his apartment. He said nobody had ever asked him that question, adding that if he had known in advance what he would undergo, he would have declined treatment.

Having just declined further chemotherapy, Tony said he felt relieved, and he sounded relieved. He assured me his affairs were in order, the distribution of his possessions clearly laid out right down to who would receive which books from his personal library. "You know, Hawley-bird," he said, "there really isn't anything more I have to do!" As that thought registered, I was aware of something like envy. Tony had that gift.

I asked when I could come to see him and was pleased that he seemed willing to get together. We agreed that I would meet him for dinner there in Boston the following week. As usual, his calendar was loaded. The date we settled on was the first evening he was free. Not wanting to tire him, I declined his invitation to stay the night in his guest room. We arranged an early dinner, after which I would continue down to the Cape to lodge with my daughter and her family.

Two good months.

A Friend Who is Also an Eminence

For at least half of the fifty years I knew him, Tony was, in addition to being my great friend and closest confidant, an undeniable eminence. We grew close as we started our teaching lives together at Cleveland's University School in the late sixties. Tony came to the school in 1967, but only part time, the year before I did. Newly ordained, he was then a beginning curate at St. Paul's Episcopal Church, a prosperous parish in suburban Cleveland Heights. Youthful, handsome, and charismatic, he immediately established a burgeoning youth program the likes of which the St. Paul's congregation had not seen before, offering after school and weekend activities to teenagers all over the east side of Cleveland, including many outside the parish, including non-Episcopalians and non-Christians.

Tony liked to tell the story of his unconventional hiring at the school. He had been asked to attend a high school soccer game in which two of his youth group regulars were playing. Both of them were University School boys. Tony's cheering them on from the sidelines caught the attention of Rowland McKinley, the school's headmaster. A noted banterer, McKinley inquired why the Church (Tony was wearing his clerical collar) had been called forth to support the University School side; Tony looked too young to be any of the boys' father. Tony responded something to the effect that the Lord works in strange ways his wonders to perform. Thus charmed, McKinley, after only a few cursory questions, offered Tony a job. Tony explained that he was already employed full time—and given Tony's inclinations, more than full time—at St. Paul's. McKinley countered by proposing just a single course, possibly two.

What McKinley didn't know, but perhaps sensed, was that Tony was dying to teach. His preparation of St. Paul's communicants and his mentoring relation-ship to the other children in his parish were what sus-tained him. With as little deliberation as McKinley had taken in proposing the job, Tony accepted on the spot. The courses he proposed, both "electives" for the up-per grades, were Anthropology and Psychology, an-thropology because the school's social studies program offered no other course in the social sciences; psychol-ogy because Tony had been reading a lot of Freud and was fascinated. Though a graduate of both Harvard and Cambridge Universities and then the Episcopal Divinity School where he was ordained, Tony had not, I believe, ever taken a course in either anthropology or psychology, but such was his resolve to begin teaching. As he reckoned, he had been on a reading tear, mainly psychology and French existential novels, and he was certain those texts and others that he loved could be carpentered into courses called Anthropology and Psychology. In the event, both courses were enthusiastically subscribed, and no one complained.

The following autumn I joined Tony on the University School faculty. I was in the process of completing the course work for a master's degree at Case Western Reserve University when a friend told me about a job opening teaching history at University School. I was twenty-three years old and feeling a special urgency to find a job, as I had just proposed marriage, and would soon need to provide the means to support us both. My undergraduate and graduate studies had been mainly in political science and philosophy. Like Tony, I had little preparation to teach anything like the courses that needed to be taught in the school's history sequence, but like him I was undaunted in my willingness to wing it. At the time, like many of my contemporaries, I was held in thrall by the work of the media sociologist Marshall McCluhan, who, it seemed to me, was saying that understanding *anything* required understanding media, and since I had caught at least the gist of what he was proposing, I thought I could bring McCluhan's vision to the study of history, or so I proposed to a dazed but receptive Headmaster McKinley.

One Friday evening a few weeks into that first hectic school year, my wife and I were heading into the school to see the high school boys' annual Variety Show, when I felt a firm clap on my shoulder and turned around to see Tony Jarvis. Because of his part time schedule, he entered and left the school only for the time it took to teach his courses before heading back to St. Paul's. We had not previously met. As he introduced himself and told me what he did at the school, I was confused, because he was wearing a dark suit and a clerical collar, and I could not reconcile my experience of the school to date with anything ecclesiastical. Nonetheless this new colleague was disarmingly cordial. He asked if he might sit with us, and I had a strong sense that I was about to make a friend.

I would go on to work at University School for almost four decades, the last seventeen as its Headmaster, but the five years I served in the traces with Tony were my vocational foundation.

When I began teaching that first year—four eighth

grade Civics classes, two ninth grade Western Civilization classes—I learned that the opening I had filled on the faculty was due to the death the previous spring of the History/Social Studies department chairman. In consequence there was a temporary hiatus in department leadership, which for me meant starting my work with, literally, no guidance. A week or so before the fall term began I was able to learn, from the business office, what books had been ordered for my courses. From a quick scan of these I set about designing a syllabus of daily lessons. I was also at the time, technically, a full-time graduate student, completing a book length master's thesis, due in February. Looking back from my present perspective, I don't think it is possible to assess the stress of that first year of teaching, the condition made endurable by the stimulation of getting to know the boys and the pleasure of getting to know some of my colleagues. My wife was at the time finishing her undergraduate training at the Cleveland Institute of Art, and with our wedding gift VW bus, we managed to get each other to our respective obligations. Of my home life, I recall mainly rushed morning and evening meals.

Of my school life, I remember fits of self-reproach on days when one or more of my classes had gone airless and flat and, less frequently, moments of elation when a day's classes felt alive with good questions and productive argument. At year's end, the boys in my classes seem to have accepted me as a credible teacher. Some of them and some of their parents made an effort to thank me. If there were concerns about my performance, nobody told me. In any event, I was reappointed with a modest, and I believe standard, salary increase. It was more than a surprise when one day in July Headmaster McKinley telephoned me to ask if I would assume the chairmanship of the department. As I would learn over the course of the following year, there was a curious admixture of eccentricity and warring views among the other history and social studies teachers that made the appointment of any of my more senior colleagues problematic. I felt more wary than honored by my elevation to this new post, about which my only instruction was to hold departmental meetings and to produce minutes which were to be submitted to the Upper School director. There had been no such meetings over the course of my first year.

I had not reckoned that I was now Tony's department chairman, the oddness of which he took generous care not to notice. In fact, he was a saving presence at the department meetings I was required to hold, meetings the previous year's "acting" chairman had refused to call on the grounds that he and, he believed, the others in the department felt were a waste of their time. That being the case, I was neither comfortable nor at all confident summoning the department to meet. It helped a little that there were some actual issues to resolve. The department's required and elective courses seemed to me substantial enough in content, but no prior attention had been given how they related to each other or how, if sequenced differently, they might build on one another. That we actually managed to conduct some useful business was due in large part to Tony's taking it—and me—seriously.

After a full year of reviewing our history curriculum, it was determined that the Western Civilization course required of all ninth graders needed to be reconstituted. The course had been a year-long march through the chapters of a single textbook, *Earlier Ages* by joint authors James Henry Breasted, Emma Robinson, and James Harvey. The earlier ages spanned prehistory through the England's loss of the American colonies. The narrative tone was pitched a few degrees higher than most ninth graders could hear. As one of the teachers assigned to teach it, I became quickly aware that it was no ninth grader's favorite course.

The following year, Tony's third at the school, he signed on to teach full time, a heartening development for me, but a demanding one for Tony, as he had become busier than ever with his parish responsibilities at St. Paul's. Tony had been an ardent student of European history both at Harvard where he had been a history major and at Cambridge where he focused on the Catholic Restoration in England. He was eager to help remake the Western Civilization course, and thus began the most rewarding academic partnership of my teaching life. We determined to abandon a single text and create instead a sequence of readings and documents that we thought might bring to life some of the defining moments in the cultures studied as well as introducing past eras' greatest ideas, greatest art, and greatest lives. This meant of course a terrific imposition of personal values on our parts, but I think for both of us, the process of deciding what was essential and what was not in the historical record was nothing less than thrilling. Over the years Tony and I would often talk about putting together the new Western Civilization course. I think we both realized that in composing and revising its content, we were clarifying who we were and what we most cared about.

And so it was that *Earlier Ages* was supplanted by a

short, beautifully illustrated history of Ancient Egypt; passages of Old and New Testament Scripture; biblical themes illustrated by contemporary reflections, including Eli Wiesel's holocaust memoir, *Night*; the trial and death dialogs of Socrates; *Oedipus Rex;* Plutarch's lives of selected Greeks and Romans; Robert Payne's *Ancient Rome*; selected lives of the saints; Einhard's *Life of Charlemagne;* Roland Bainton's life of Martin Luther; Jean Anouilh' *Becket;* Robert Massie's *Nicholas and Alexandra.*

We knew we were post holing through the centuries, and when we needed texts to tie certain periods together, we wrote them ourselves.

It was important to Tony that we learn what the boys themselves made of the new course—and indeed all of the courses taught in the department, so we began the process of anonymous year end student course evaluations. In a year or two it was clear: Western Civilization had become, in the boys' view, the most challenging and "favorite" ninth grade course. Between preparing the new classes and teaching them, I know I have never worked harder, and I am certain Tony felt the same. From Tony I also learned what it meant to have a colleague. We were competitive, but in the best possible way. We couldn't wait to tell each other highlights and low points of our classes. I remember the afternoon Tony popped into my office to show me a passage one of his students (I still remember his name) had written about the price the Israelites had to pay for "whoreshipping false idols." We read each other's student exams, observed each other's classes. We did our best to incorporate anything the other was doing that worked especially well. Proctoring exams together at the end of a term, we would whisper historical trivia questions to each other. The name of Alexander the Great's horse? *Bucephalus*!

My fourth year at the school I was given a leave of absence to attend Cambridge University in order to write my doctoral thesis, which proposed a value-based approach to the concept of the public interest. To complete it, I needed a grounding in theological ethics, which Case Western University could not provide. It was Tony who suggested Cambridge where he had studied, at St. John's College, after his graduation from Harvard. So off I went, also to St. John's. It was a rich year in more ways than I can relate here, and I remember feeling grateful that I entered that scholastic world in my mid-twenties, because had I been younger I would have been, being who I was, overwhelmed by both Cambridge's scholarly expectations and the complexity of the university culture. Before I departed to the UK, Tony took pains to tell me what I might expect and plied me with books about Cambridge history and architecture—to the extent that when my wife and I made our way out of the Cambridge rail station into the city proper, I had an eerie sensation that I was somehow returning.

Tony and I corresponded regularly over the course of my time at Cambridge, and I was grateful for his impressions of what was going on at school. One such development was that he had replaced me as chairman of the history department, which seemed to me more than appropriate. I had made it known that when I returned I hoped I might take on some kind of role in student guidance and discipline. After a good deal of back and forth with various administrators, it was determined that I would be Dean of Students, a new position at the upper school. In it I would monitor the faculty-student advisory system, work individually with troubled students, and participate in discipline decisions, in addition to teaching Western Civilization and elective courses to students in the upper grades.

It was bracing to resume my duties that fall, especially to continue working with Tony on the Western Civilization project. While we were still very much teaching partners, Tony had emerged as a forceful and directive chairman of the department. I had briefly been chairman myself, but I did not know what it was like to be served by a good one.

University School's Upper School campus was then just two years old, a modernist brick and glass school house settled in a recess of a three hundred acre forest in exurban Hunting Valley, Ohio. The building was distinctive for admitting a great deal of natural light and for vast carpeted expanses of open space. The classrooms were unadorned rectangles with white metal walls and acoustic tile ceilings. The only visual feature in these identical rooms was a green chalkboard. We met our classes in whatever room was assigned to us; none us had our "own" classroom. Because the Western Civilization sections were assigned the same room, Tony took it upon himself to mount pictures and documents on its walls, most of the materials purchased at his own expense.

The classroom I returned to that autumn featured a desk-level to ceiling montage of images of the pyramids of Gizeh, the treasures of King Tut's Tomb, aerial views of the Nile Delta and of the cataracts to the south, diagrams of hieroglyphics and of various aspects of tomb-building technology and construction. It was the most visually rich classroom I had ever seen, and Tony had put it together himself over the summer. There was no other classroom like it in the school. The metallic walls were designed to be reconfigured to create alternative spaces, and it was not easy to mount anything on them, so most of the other classrooms were unadorned. Appreciative as I was to renew my teaching in this visually lively space, I had not expected that every time the school resumed after an end-of-term or holiday break, Tony would have recreated the display to illustrate the themes we would be covering in the weeks ahead. It is hard to describe the impact of this extra effort and attention on Tony's part. I would go on to teach the World War II holocaust for decades, but never, after my first year back from Cambridge, without picturing and *feeling* the presence of the archival prints Tony had mounted of Jews of the Warsaw ghetto looking up warily from their daily business, of serious looking Jewish children clasping satchels of their belongings as they waited at rail sidings for what was unthinkable. Many of the children pictured looked to be the age of the boys in my class.

The attention to the Western Civilization classroom is only one example of the care Tony took with the history and social studies program. Before his assuming the chairmanship, films had occasionally, but not frequently, been screened in certain classes in the humanities. One reason for the infrequency was that feature length films were too long for a typical classroom period. Another reason was that the technology for showing films at the time was eight or sixteen-millimeter projectors that had to be hand threaded with sprocketed reels of celluloid film, a skill only a few of the boys and almost none of the faculty had mastered. Undeterred, Tony spent nearly one full summer identifying, previewing, and ordering dozens of excellent educational films, almost all of them produced by Encyclopedia Britannica, for not just the Western Civilization course but also for American History and other courses offered by the department.

As much as I benefitted from it, visual and audio-visual enhancement was far from the hallmark of Tony's presence among our departmental colleagues. He wanted us to think about how and what we taught. We had at the time long established, imperturbable colleagues who were not reluctant to dismiss any pedagogical "latest thing" or the person championing it. Tony was able to get past their reflexive resistance by agreeing with them, while pointing out what elements of various reforms might actually be grounded in what has always constituted good teaching. As our chairman,

Tony insisted that we meet, that we review what we were doing and could defend it. He invited us to *argue,* and none of us for a moment doubted where he stood on most issues.

In the five years we worked together at University School Tony taught me two things that shaped my approach to school life ever afterward. "Taught" is maybe not quite right, although I learned these things from him; more precisely, like Tom Sawyer painting his fence, Tony made the necessary, often invisible work of teaching feel admirable, even heroic. He was, for example, a meticulous and prompt grader of papers, his neatly written comments and corrections in red a respectful tribute to the work submitted. The boys' unarticulated response to the care he took was something like "if *he* cares this much about my paper/test/quiz, maybe I should."

Tony had somehow reconciled with his diocesan superiors that he could retain his considerable responsibilities as Associate Rector of St. Paul's while carrying on as a fully committed teacher and administrator at University School. At the time, I could only guess how Tony managed to juggle and balance his duties on both fronts. Given his still active direction of the St. Paul's youth program and participation, including preaching, in Sunday services, he had little time for school work on the weekends and absolutely no time to relax and decompress. He seemed never to miss the school's Saturday athletic contests, which often commenced mid-morning and proceeded through late afternoon. I cannot remember entering the school in the morning and not seeing Tony sitting in his office, a small desk lamp illuminating the otherwise dark surrounding space, inscribing comments onto stacks of exams books or papers. Otherwise cordial and effusive during the school day, he made it clear in these before-school encounters that he was racing to complete his work before his classes began and was not to be interrupted. When I left school at day's end after a late meeting or an athletic practice, the picture was the same: Tony at his desk by the lamp, red pen poised above an exam book.

I too had what always felt like too many papers and tests to grade, a condition that even now casts approaching Sundays with a vague sense of dread. But working alongside Tony, it felt intolerable—shameful—not at least to try to work as hard as he did. My overall impression of Tony then and in the years to follow was that in whatever role he was cast, *he did the work.*

That work included close attention to details. Tony kept his appointments, remembered dates, showed up at students' and parishioners' bar mitzvahs, confirmations, Eagle Scout inductions. If it fell to him to introduce a speaker or welcome a guest to the school, he took care to find out the guest's background and notable achievements before composing eloquent remarks of welcome. I observed this remarkable attention to particulars in the succession of distinguished academic and ecclesiastical positions he would go on to assume. Whether presiding over a school banquet or an annual Headmasters Association conference, Tony specified the seating, setting, and other appointments for every room in which business was conducted. With respect to meals served, Tony selected every item on offer and composed its description for the embossed printed menus that would appear at each place setting. On the arrival of visitors from abroad and on established holidays, appropriate flags were hoisted above the main entrance of his school.

As we became friends that first year at University School, he would counter my wonder that he could be so busy on so many fronts by saying he was a bachelor with no dependents. He said he had more time than I did. He also lived what seemed to me to be very simply: a small, rather spartan apartment close to the school, rooms minimally furnished with odds and ends, but lots of books. Like mine, his salary was modest, as were his expenses. Nonetheless, even in those first years, neither of us making $7,000 a year, Tony insisted on picking up every check for everything from a stop for coffee to a full restaurant meal. This practice continued on well past the time any consideration of "Well, you have a wife and family to support" made practical sense. Only occasionally was I able to treat Tony to a meal—or to anything else: theater tickets, parking fees, cab fares—and then only by some clandestine prearrangement with maître d'. I have never known a person more compulsively generous than Tony.

That Tony was, to my mind, impossibly over-committed to his two callings never registered to me as a burden grimly borne. His outward manner was alternately exuberant and determined. He was terrific company. He reveled in taking extreme positions and inviting you to disagree. He had an easy and often irreverent sense of humor and none of the reserve people might associate with clerics. Without being cruel, he liked to banter, and his favorite tropes were mock insults and wild exaggeration. If he wanted to praise a poem I had just shown him, he was apt to say, "Hawley-bird"—I can't remember when he started calling me Hawley-bird, but it might have been immediately—"that is the best poem ever written in English." When we disagreed on a book or film, he might say, "I can't believe you sat through ten minutes of that abomination. You have by far the worst taste of anybody I have ever met." These pronouncements were always uttered while smiling broadly. He took even greater pleasure when extravagant insults were directed back at him, even from the boys. I would estimate that more than half the time we were together was spent laughing.

What surprised and impressed me most as I was getting to know Tony was that, in addition his clear competence at what he set himself to do, he was restlessly creative. The second year we taught together, he popped over to visit one afternoon bearing a folder of papers. He said he had started a book project, a scripture-based life of Jesus he thought he could use both in his communicant classes at St. Paul's and in our Western Civilization course—and would I mind reviewing his chapters as he wrote them. He knew that I had writing aspirations, mostly poetry at the time, and would I make whatever suggestions and corrections that occurred to me. I was flattered to be asked and also curious about what kind of life of Christ Tony thought would appeal to early teenagers, including many non-Christians.

Thus began a weekly exchange of manila folders,

his to me with a new chapter, mine back to him with my edits and suggestions. Our collaboration continued throughout that school year, and I found it stimulating. A good deal of the text was extended passages of the Gospels, preceded and followed by Tony's clearly written explications. The tone of Tony's prose was direct and welcoming, and he managed to avoid proselytizing, or even advocacy, by opening up narrated events—accounts of miraculous healing, the virgin birth, the resurrection—to critical questioning by citing the positions taken by both sceptics and the faithful. I had only dim Sunday School recollection of the Gospel stories, and I learned a great deal from my weekly close reading of Tony's chapters. For his part, Tony was effusively grateful for my comments and corrections. By spring of that year he had secured a publishing contract for the book, now titled *And Still is Ours Today* (a refrain from a Protestant hymn "Now Thank We all our God"), from Seabury Press. The book was ready for us to use with our students the following winter. The boys found it accessible and engaging. I found it a pleasure to teach, and I was not alone in this. The book got strong reviews from both educational and Christian journals, and it sold sufficiently well that Seabury offered Tony a second contract to write a similar treatment of the entire Old Testament. Tony and I collaborated in the same manner on what a year later would become *Prophets, Poets, Priests, and Kings,*" also well received and a staple of the Western Civilization course for every year I taught it.

Working on these projects with Tony became an integral part of my learning to be a teacher. In both books' prefaces Tony acknowledged my contribution generously. In all, the experience was formative. The idea that you could *own*, that you could *create* what you teach went deep with me. Also, Tony's methodical and undramatic approach to composition convinced me that with sufficient discipline and focus a teacher could be a writer—that *I* could be a writer.

In more ways than I can recount here, Tony's mastery of the material he taught and his manner of presenting it were an inspiration. He was warm and direct with his students. You could not stand outside his classroom for five minutes without hearing the boys erupt in laughter. He traded banter about the boys' athletics and out-of-school lives. He was the only teacher at that time who did not mind being addressed by his first name, but this did not detract from the respectful and purposeful atmosphere he maintained in both his Western Civilization classes and his eagerly subscribed

Philosophy elective for upper classmen. The boys re- garded him as especially rigorous but fair—and fun.

Admirable and inspiring as Tony was as a teacher, he taught me another, more valuable lesson in the years we worked together in Cleveland. Like many indepen- dent schools, University School had a faculty-student advisory system. A few weeks into each school year, boys were asked to indicate, in order of preference, three of their teachers they would like to serve as what we called faculty "sponsors." Sponsors were to serve as confidants to their sponsees and as mediators with oth- er teachers and the administration if problems arose. In addition, faculty sponsors wrote letters to parents twice a year summarizing their sponsees' progress through the school. Because we wanted to honor the boys' pref- erences, we did our best to match them with their first choices, assigning second and, more rarely, third choic- es only when the teachers they preferred were already oversubscribed. The policy of honoring the boys' pref- erences inevitably resulted in inequities in the number of sponsees faculty would serve. I remember feeling heartened when a larger than average number of boys was assigned to me, despite the extra work entailed; it was impossible not to feel affirmed by being chosen. On the other hand, colleagues assigned just a few sponsees or, very occasionally, none, could not help feeling hurt. Most of my colleagues made honorable attempts to form helpful relationships with the boys they served as sponsor. I remember being startled to learn that Tony had been assigned—and agreed to take on—more than twice the number of sponsees assigned to anyone else.

Tony was attentive to his sponsees, and it was instructive to see how a variety of boys flourished because of that attention. But unlike any other colleague at the time, Tony extended himself to any boy in the school who seemed lost or lonely, but especially to the handful of boys who were considered scholastic or behavioral disasters. It was often the case that these were personally unhappy boys who were acting out in desperation. I found some of these boys hard to know and even harder to like. Tony sought them out, whether they were his own students or not. He talked to them privately. He tutored them in free periods and after school. He was at once their worst nightmare and best friend; their worst nightmare because he confronted them with their behavior, their defenses, their vulnerability; their best friend because they came to know he had no reason to intrude into their lives except that he cared about them. He seemed to be certain that, despite all outward evidence, they were good, promising, valuable people. And of course when that kind of gift is given, boys change. They improve. And, as Tony came to know over the course of a long career, such boys do not forget the gift they were given. Tony spent six years on the faculty of University School; dozens of the boys he taught and counseled there remained in relationship to him throughout his life. Decades later, I greeted many of them who had traveled across the country and even overseas to attend Tony's funeral Mass.

University School, when we worked there together, was as secular as a private school was likely to be at the time. It was not a religious foundation to begin with, and our headmaster, though in other ways lovable, was profoundly uncomfortable with any kind of formal worship. Moreover, the school was a hearty mix of Protestants, Roman Catholics, Jews, sceptics, and non-believers. Into this mix, Tony wore his clerical garb to school every day. He reintroduced prayer at shared meals. One notable Easter week, he scripted a version of Christ's passion, in which the whole assembled Upper School took part as vocal participants. Tony cast me as Jesus, not, I think, due to his regard for any Christ-like qualities in me, but more likely in the hopes of somehow improving me. He cast our headmaster as Pontius Pilate. As it happened, all of us, faculty and boys alike, were energized by what was a highly liturgical exercise. Nobody complained. Tony could do that.

In other ways, too, if hard to describe with precision, Tony helped to realize what was an especially rich and unsettling time for University School. In the late sixties and early seventies the emergent youth culture was challenging longstanding cultural norms ranging from civil decorum to personal appearance to sexual practices. Some of my colleagues and all of my students were eager witnesses. Our headmaster and other administrators did an admirable job welcoming opposing viewpoints to address the school: elected officials, Viet Nam resisters, black power advocates, proponents of alternative schooling. Through all of it, Tony managed to introduce his own distinctive viewpoint and concerns. He arranged a screening and all-day reflection on Malcolm Muggeridge's documentary film, "Something Beautiful for God," about Mother Teresa's mission to the poor of Calcutta. Some of the books he assigned to the students in his philosophy elective were so energetically discussed and argued about that other students and faculty wanted in on the consideration of Viktor Frankl's *Man's Search for Meaning,* Jean Paul Sartre's *Nausea*, and John Farrow's *Damien the Leper.* Even those who moved farthest from

Tony's orbit in the course of a school day were struck by the young man with the clerical collar, whom some of the boys called "Tony," who seemed to have urgent things to say. I don't think anyone who shared the years of Tony's tenure at University School would disagree with my sense that his presence was a defining element of that unforgettable time.

In the winter of 1974 I got a sense that something was going on with Tony. He seemed uncharacteristically distracted as he went about his daily business at school. On two consecutive weekends he told me he would be unavailable because he was going out of town. The second of those weekends he asked our headmaster if he could add a day to his weekend stay. Only when he returned from that long weekend did he call me into his office to explain. He had just been offered, and had accepted, the headmastership of The Roxbury Latin School, a small independent boys' school in Boston. My response to the news was complicated. I did not know he was looking to work elsewhere; he had told only our headmaster and had asked him to tell nobody until and unless there was something to tell. I also felt an enormous pang of loss. Tony had not only become a close friend; I felt we were partners in forging a fresh approach to teaching and counseling at the school. It was hard for me to picture the school without Tony in it.

There was much to process for me as we talked, and I probably did not take in everything he told me about the school he had been chosen to lead. He did convey that he really liked some of its features, that it was small, with about 270 boys in grades seven through twelve, and that it was steeped in the classics, offering both Latin and Greek. He was especially impressed that the school was ancient. He must have told me how ancient, but only later did I learn that Roxbury Latin was founded in 1645 and was the oldest school in continuous operation in the United States.

As we talked, Tony was uncharacteristically tentative. He did not sound elated at having landed a big new job. Looking back, this may have been the only time he ever gave me an impression that he was a little lost. He went on to say that the trustees who interviewed him told him that there was a good deal of work to be done by the new headmaster. A handsome old schoolhouse had fallen into disrepair. The classical curriculum had not been supported by the departing headmaster, and, in the tradition-challenging spirit of the day, the need even to offer classical languages had been called into question. From what Tony said, it sounded as if the school, like most independent schools at the time, was questioning established practices with an eye to less confining, more liberating reforms. He said the school didn't seem to have dress code, and the general school climate felt a little rackety. The problems ahead had nothing to do with money, Tony said. Small though it was, the school had over the centuries amassed a sufficient endowment, millions more than University School's, and we were three times Roxbury Latin's size.

As I listened, I realized how much I was going to miss him, but I was also impressed—that he was even aware of headmasterships opening up in distant cities, that faraway schools somehow knew about Tony Jarvis. And a *headmaster*. My regard for the position was already elevated by coming to know my own distinctive and nationally prominent headmaster, Rowland McKinley. Within a few weeks of our acquaintance, Tony began giving me books about headmasters and their schools, including his favorite, a book he said that helped him decide to be a priest: *Peabody of Groton*, written by Frank Ashburn, himself a revered headmaster of the Brooks School north of Boston. But Tony *himself* as a headmaster. He didn't seem to me old enough. He was thirty-four but looked younger. His energy seemed to me youthful energy.

I don't think Tony himself was sure if he was old enough. In an oddly confessional tone, he asked me please not to tell anyone, but on the flight home from Boston after he had been confidentially assured he would be named the next headmaster of Roxbury Latin, he had drunk three of the little airplane bottles of vodka. I couldn't picture it. Tony rarely had a drink, and when he did, he had only one. "I would have had more," he said, "but the plane landed." He said he could barely find his apartment door when he got out of the cab. I think he was telling me that committing himself to this new calling in a new place hadn't settled in him yet. He also confided that even though he had been invited back for a final interview, he did not think he would be offered the job. In fact, he said, he was sure this was so after his answer to the last question he was asked: "Mr. Jarvis, what is your personal vision for the school, should you be asked to head it?"

Tony said he didn't even pause to consider: "I would like to create a community of love." He said the room fell silent, and then he was excused so that the board could deliberate. "I was sure I had blown it," he said. We chatted and laughed for a while longer as the event settled.

HEADMASTER

At the start of the fall term midway through Tony's thirty-year tenure as Headmaster of the Roxbury Latin School, he rose from his chair on the stage of the darkly paneled Rousmaniere Hall and moved to the lectern to welcome back the boys and staff who, decorously and in unison, had just seated themselves. The boys ranged from the undersized, wide eyed sixth class, or "sixies," for whom this was their first day of Roxbury Latin, to rangy seniors who were outwardly indistinguishable from younger faculty. For all but the new boys, this was a familiar moment in a familiar place. Headmaster Jarvis addressed the assembled school often from this stage, and always at the beginning of each of the three terms of the school year. The talks were serious and decidedly long, especially for boys looking forward to greeting old friends and sizing up their new classes. But they would be attentive, because Mr. Jarvis invariably said things that surprised them, and when he had finished, many of them would feel challenged in a way they would have a hard time putting into words.

Their headmaster regarded them silently for a moment and then began:

One night this past vacation I came to realize afresh that no segment of the population is more lied to than adolescents. Last Tuesday night, after a particularly grueling sequence of days and nights, I crawled home for a late supper and—foolish optimist that I am—I grabbed the weekly TV guide and looked eagerly for something that would entertain me on my first night of TV in months. I recognized nothing on the schedule, but after perusing the blurbs under 8 P.M. I settled on "Who's the Boss?" It was a charming little story about a dumb but lovable father who found it hard to trust his teenage daughter to go on a date. Upshot, father falsely accuses daughter, daughter is innocent, father apologizes, much hugging.

Done in by this gripping drama I was too weak to change channels and soon found myself done in by the epic that followed at 8:30: "Growing Pains." The subject of this story was a dumb but lovable teenage son who decides to take a part-time job with a former buddy who is a bad guy. Upshot: son takes job, son realizes former buddy is a bad guy, son comes home to worried, trusting parents to tell them that they (the trusting parents) were right all along. Much hugging.

As I watched I suddenly realized that these two shows

have been playing on TV for at least thirty-five years, only under different names—Ozzie and Harriet, Flipper, My Three Sons, The Brady Bunch, The Partridge Family, Eight is Enough, to name a few from the recent past. American audiences never tire of these two relentlessly and endlessly recurring plots: parents come to realize their kids are basically good and then apologize for not trusting them; kids who come to realize their parents' values are right and then apologize for doubting their loving parents.

Both these plots are reassuring and I predict your children and grandchildren will watch them reenacted on TV (or whatever replaces TV) for years to come. Why, then, make a big deal about them?

The reason I make a big deal about them is that they oversimplify life's complexity to such a degree that they are lies— quite damaging lies about the way life really is…

…Real parents usually are not cute and lovable, they have serious problems of their own, they have to earn a living, they have to deal with disappointments, they are not always there, they can't always understand. Conflicts are rarely resolved in twenty-two minutes (thirty minutes minus eight minutes for commercials) and sometimes never resolved at all. Real adolescents are usually not very cute and lovable, they have zits and body odor, they aren't always surrounded by pals or by adoring members of the opposite

sex, they make bad mistakes with long-range consequences, they don't get out of every scrape unscathed, they don't resolve disagreements neatly, they don't get all their hurts nicely and immediately nursed. Family fights do not always end in hugging… Real parents and real adolescents are not like that. Life is not like that.

Having introduced the "TV lie," the headmaster goes on to address "The Best-Years-of-Your-Life Lie":

…I rebuked a parent the other day for laughing about what she called the "puppy love" of her son who had broken up with his girlfriend. I rebuked her because I think such events hurt adolescents more deeply than they hurt adults who have been through them before and know they will survive. There is much about adolescence that is painful. Fortunately human beings—over time—tend to sift out unhappy memories and remember the good things about the past. That's what an adult is doing who tells you, "These are the happiest days of your life." But whatever tricks memory may play, the reality is that adolescence is not the happiest time of life—but rather a time of often painful self-discovery, of confusion about who you are and what you want, of self-doubt, fear of failure, and dread of rejection.

I thought I was pretty happy as a teenager, but I have

found the years after adolescence far happier and more fulfilling. And I believe you will.

And the "There Should Be No Pain Lie":

Parents sometimes say to me, "You don't realize how terribly hurt my son was to be cut from the team," or a variation, "I'm worried about his self-image; you don't realize how hurt he was to get so little playing time." But I do realize—because I was bitterly disappointed on both counts myself as a teenager. I was cut and I sat on the bench, and in retrospect I probably learned more from those "defeats" than I learned from my successes. I had to dig deep and find self-respect. And doing so has prepared me well for all the defeats and reverses adult life dishes out to everyone.

...It may well be that the most valuable experiences we have in adolescence are not our triumphs or our successes or our popularity, but rather our disappointments and defeats and rejections. We grow more through our sufferings than through our successes.

There is a good deal more than quoted above about what Tony had to say about the "lies" adults are inclined to tell children. He spoke at even greater length about what he hoped the boys listening might do about the inevitable troubles and failings that lay ahead of them. He offered solutions ranging from better personal organization to seeking the consolation of others, concluding with the healing power of prayer.

There is much in life that we are not in complete control of—much that we have to offer up. That's what prayer is: the crying out, the offering up of the mess we're in. "I don't know if I can hack this. I don't know a way out of this mess. Help!"

At the conclusion of his talk, the boys had been listening for nearly forty minutes, with little observable sign of restlessness or boredom. As the sixies would come to understand, this was Roxbury Latin. Their headmaster's concluding case for the healing power of prayer would not surprise them, nor would the offering of specific prayers and blessings. In back-to-school assemblies and other occasions throughout the school year, they would hear committed expressions of faith—of all faiths—from their headmaster, from invited guests to the school, and from boys themselves. Roxbury Latin, though established as a "free School" for the children of colonial "Roxburie," was not a sectarian or even specifically Christian foundation. Established by the Puritan divine John Eliot, renowned as "apostle to the Indians" of colonial Massachusetts, the school's 1645 charter stated:

Whereas the Inhabitantes of Roxburie, out of their religious care of posteritie, have taken into consideration how necessarie the Education of theire children in Literature will fit them for publick service in both Churche and Commonwealthe, in succeeding ages; They therefore unanimously have consented and agreed to erect a free schoole in the said towne of Roxburie.

Over the centuries to follow, the "religious care of posteritie" would gradually recede from the school's mission in favor of rigorous instruction in the classics, arts, and sciences, to the point that by the mid twentieth century both the scholastic program and culture of the school had become entirely secular. With the 1974 appointment of the Rev. F. Washington Jarvis as headmaster, that culture would be reconsidered and changed.

The talk Tony delivered that morning was one of ninety start-of-term addresses he would give over three decades at the school and one of forty-two collected in the book *With Love and Prayers* published by David Godine in 2000. The presumable market for such a book would be the families and graduates of Roxbury Latin, but enthusiastic word-of-mouth endorsements from initial readers led to a more general readership, to the extent that in 2001 the book and its author were honored with a Christopher Award. Christopher Awards were established in 1949 to recognize works in any medium—theater, television, books—that "affirm the highest values of the human spirit." Tony Jarvis was honored at the 2001 ceremony along with the folk singer and memoirist Judy Collins and Fred Rogers, "Mister Rogers" of children's television.

In his introduction to *With Love and Prayers*, Peter Gomes, Plummer Professor of Christian Morals at the Harvard Divinity School and Pusey Minister at Harvard Memorial Church, began, "The Reverend F. Washington Jarvis and The Roxbury Latin School over which he has presided for a quarter of a century are each anachronisms and proud of so-being; and in the crowded field of private secondary education in North America both stand out because neither fits in." Gomes, a life trustee of the school and a good friend of Tony's, went on to celebrate the misfit for his courage, for his clarity, and his transformative effect on what had become by any objective measure an excellent school.

TAKING CHARGE

Concluding his address to the school with a case for the efficacy of prayer and asking for help was not a pious bromide for Tony. He had not yet settled into his new position as Roxbury Latin's headmaster in the fall of 1974 when he experienced his own prayerful need for help. From his initial visits to the school, he had made a hopeful assessment. The school's strong suits were obvious. The endowment per pupil was so strong that admission could be offered to families for thousands of dollars less than the fees required at competing private schools. As a result, bright and otherwise promising boys from families of modest means continued to seek out Roxbury Latin. Despite signs of flagging enrollment, worrying attrition, and a related softening of the school's scholastic rigor in the decade before Tony's arrival, Roxbury Latin seniors continued to win acceptance to highly selective colleges and universities. On any given year, it was not unusual for a third of the school's graduates to be admitted to Harvard. Perhaps the single greatest factor in the school's favor, Tony believed, was that it was relatively small. With rarely more than 300 boys in six grades, it was possible for everybody in the community, boy and adult, to know one another. It was a school in which it might be possible that, in the words Tony would later insert into the school's published prospectus, "every boy is known and loved."

The combination of Roxbury Latin's venerable age, tradition of rigor, and its classical curriculum was in many ways a dream come true for Tony. Though to some extent aligned with the inter-generational conflicts of the day—he had actively opposed the war in Viet Nam and championed civil rights—he recognized in Roxbury Latin a largely intact remnant of the British grammar schools on which it had earlier been modeled. And as his new colleagues would soon realize, their new headmaster was as devoted an Anglophile as he was a Christian.

Even before he presided over the opening exercises of his new school in the fall of 1974, Tony was aware that he was entering a more troubled school community than he had been led to believe. A year prior, the trustees had asked for the resignation of its headmaster of eight years, Richmond Mayo-Smith, on the grounds that the school had veered too far off its traditional foundation. A committed educational progressive, Mayo-Smith had granted both faculty and students more autonomy to decide what was taught and how it would be taught. The interim head assigned to replace Mayo-Smith while the board searched for a permanent head was a much beloved history teacher and coach, Bill Chauncey. Tony and Chauncey hit it off on first meeting, and while their relationship would progress into a lifelong friendship, its warmth did little to prepare Tony for what had become a faculty sorely divided between those allied to the school's traditional rigor and those who felt liberated by their recently granted discretion as to how they conducted their classes, discretion that, Tony discovered to his astonishment, extended to whether or not teachers could dismiss students before the scheduled time allotted—or whether, for one reason or another, they could call off a class altogether. Mayo-Smith had determined to abandon a faculty dress code, though he said he personally preferred coat and tie. The boys were understandably glad to be relieved of many former requirements, including, for the older boys, the requirement to remain on school grounds through the school day. The faculty that greeted Headmaster Jarvis in the autumn of 1974 was uneasily divided, and the newly liberated student body was on edge awaiting the arrival of the priest in clerical collar from Cleveland, Ohio, who would soon take charge of them.

In August of that year, I called Tony to see how he was getting along in his new situation, and while he had much to report, there was a distinct tone of concern in his voice. He had that day been confronted by one of his new young colleagues who objected to Tony's attempt to dress up the gallery at the entrance to the school. This was a passage lined with floor-to-ceiling arched windows that the building's architect, William G. Perry, had modeled after the *loggia* of the Convent of St. Mark in Florence—the kind of architectural detail Tony treasured. Headmaster Mayo-Smith, feeling the interior wall of the gallery should be lightened up, had installed cork boards on which student artwork could be featured. As Tony took the measure of the school building on his arrival that summer, he determined that little care had been taken with what was displayed on corridor and classroom walls, and he resolved to improve the look of the place. He found in attic storage a number of framed oil portraits of past Roxbury Latin worthies and took it upon himself to repair the ones that were damaged and to hang some of the others in what he had now determined was the school's *loggia.* In his young colleague's point of view and, he said, in the view of the rest of the faculty, the old portraits had been taken down for a reason. They were stodgy. They hearkened vaguely to the past. This was not a promising line to take with Tony, who hearkened longingly to the past and found great inspiration there.

As Tony progressed into the first months of the school year, a divided faculty made its preferences known. Though Mayo-Smith, the prior headmaster, had been gone for a full year, the younger faculty he hired and a few of the others fully supported the direction he had hoped to take the school. Mayo-Smith had enthusiastically embraced reforms proposed by educational theorists Jonathan Kozol (*Free Schools*, 1972) and Neil Postman (*Teaching as a Subversive Activity*, 1970), a copy of which he had distributed to his faculty and trustees. As part of what was intended to be a celebration of the school's 325th anniversary, Mayo-Smith addressed the need to focus on the future:

…*Students and teachers will relate to one another differently; students will have more autonomy. They will share initiative for planning learning activities more than they do now. Students will spend less time in class being taught by teachers; more time in conferences with teachers and students, in individual research and in learning situations sponsored by the school, but outside the school. We will begin to act on the advice from* Teaching as a Subversive Activity, *namely, the critical content of any learning experience is the method or process through which the learning occurs…It is not what you say to people that counts; it is what you have them do.*

Mayo-Smith went on to cite James Michener's vision of an educational future in which "we will soon start producing well-educated men and women to whom the book will be a minor aspect of culture. They will be visually oriented and will be just as alert as their book-oriented fellows, but they will learn intuitively, rather than solidly…"

Tony had read some of that period's educational reformers' books with interest, including *Summerhill,* the Scottish educator A. S. Neill's case for a school community in which each student determined his or her own program, including the option not to study anything at all. I can only imagine what Tony might make of "learning intuitively," but his own experience in the schools in which he studied and in the one where he had taught inclined him powerfully to favor "learning solidly."

As he proceeded into his first term as headmaster, Tony was approached by several colleagues and a few trustees to apprise him that the school's very survival was at stake if it failed to accommodate the prevailing educational and social climate of the age. He was told that in five years no one will consider attending a boys' school—

that Roxbury Latin must become coeducational. It was equally urgent, some felt, to stop requiring every student to study Latin. For financial reasons and in order to be more competitive in athletics, some coaches and trustees felt the school would benefit from expanding its enrollment. Some had embraced Mayo-Smith's preference for individualized learning over of standard classroom practices. A few faculty members let Tony know that the era of a headmaster addressing the assembled student body from the stage in a homiletic fashion had passed.

The boys of Roxbury Latin could not help being unsettled by their teachers' clashing views about whether traditional or progressive educational policies should prevail, views which to the boys often came down to strict versus lenient, hard versus easy. In the winter of 1973, when headmaster Mayo-Smith had departed and headmaster Jarvis had yet to be appointed, a fifth-year boy assessed the condition of the student body in an article for the weekly student newspaper, *Juba:*

Many changes have taken place in RL during the four and a half years I have been here. A lot of them have been for the better, but one area of life has suffered: school spirit. There is no unity in the school now; people just don't give a damn. They would rather the school fall apart or destroy it themselves, than lift a finger to help it. People have no respect for other people's rights. Books, jackets, papers, and money are stolen from their classmates; food is stolen from the lunch room; basketballs and tape recorders and books are stolen from the school. People just don't care who their deed may affect; they themselves are all-important…

This was not a school climate for which Tony Jarvis was prepared. Faculty and administrators at University School had also taken varying positions along the traditional-progressive spectrum, but there was little rancor. Headmaster McKinley tended to favor elements of both past and experimental practice, and he could be persuasive. In the years Tony and I taught together, friendship tended to mute differences in various colleagues' approaches to their work. I think both of us experienced a lively, purposeful school. Specifically, I don't think Tony was prepared for—or practiced in—confrontation. He differed, and differed openly, with some of his colleagues about matters of discipline, classroom rigor, and course content, but never combatively. Within our department and in larger curricular considerations of which he had been put in charge as Director of Studies, Tony had readily accommodated differences of opinion and approach. Strong as he could be in advocacy or criticism, I cannot recall his disapproving of or disliking anyone on the faculty. I am sure he felt, with good reason, supported and admired by the boys and his fellow teachers at University School.

Headmaster Mayo-Smith had been almost unanimously asked to resign by the Roxbury Latin trustees. A number of the younger faculty and boys who felt newly liberated and empowered by changes Mayo-Smith had implemented were resentful of the board's decision and wary of what might come next. Mayo-Smith left the school almost immediately, without the standard agreeable-sounding letters to the school community in which the departing head announces a new direction in his career, and the chairman of the board thanks him for his service. There was heated talk among confused and angry parents. *The Boston Globe* aired the unease in two extensive articles.

Tony assumed his duties knowing he would somehow have to unify the school's divisions and clarify its mission. He confided to me that he thought he might gentle the hostility of his most strident critics on the faculty by befriending them. He had high hopes working closely with the most oppositional among them might put their working relationship on a new footing. I knew Tony well enough at this point to know that he was extremely sensitive to being disliked, dismissed, disapproved of. Believing he was doing his best to promote what he felt was durable and right for not just Roxbury Latin, but for any school, he struggled with the realization that in this new setting, some of his colleagues and constituents didn't like him, attributed opinions and qualities to him he did not think he had. He let me know in a tone that worried me that all was not well. He said he was having trouble sleeping and had consulted a doctor. Troubled as he was, he could not shake the convictions that lay at the heart of his problem. Stressful as he found it, confrontation with his faculty critics only strengthened those convictions, which he was determined to declare without reservation.

He believed a boys' school rightly constituted could meet the developmental needs of adolescent boys in a way coeducated schools could not. Teachers who taught boys exclusively became, whether consciously or not, experts about how boys mature and learn. Having studied Latin himself as a student at St. Mark's School, then Greek and some Hebrew in his graduate and divinity studies, he was convinced that Roxbury Latin's classical language requirements contributed to the demonstrated scholastic excellence of its graduates. The school's classical emphasis was a distinction, not a liability. What may have attracted Tony most about the school was its intimate size and the possibility that everyone in it—boy, teacher, staff—could know one another. He saw no humane or scholastic value added by expanding the school's enrollment, and if it was expensive to maintain a small, intimate school, then that, not expansion, should be the goal of fund raising. Finally, Tony couldn't imagine *not* addressing the assembled school from the headmaster's bully pulpit. As he would make clear repeatedly in his talks to the school over the coming decades, commercial media and pop culture relentlessly convey values. It is the responsibility of schools and their leaders to mediate among those values and, where necessary, to propose better ones.

Firmly held as they were, these convictions were on a collision course with the preferences of his faculty critics. Throughout the spring of his first year and continuing into the following fall, anti-Jarvis faculty members did not conceal their views from the boys they taught or from the boys' parents. There was little of the easy-going camaraderie among colleagues that had sustained Tony in Cleveland. Over the telephone he sounded more stressed and unhappy than I had ever heard him. Knowing that without the board's support, his position at the school was unsustainable, he took care to confer regularly with each trustee individually, especially those senior members who had been designated trustees for life. He let them know the school was presently not a happy camp and what the divisive issues were. He did not want them to be surprised by complaints from unhappy constituents.

By the spring of his second year, the lingering tension had come to a dramatic head. A cadre of faculty favoring Mayo-Smith's vision for the school had not eased their resistance to their new headmaster. Specifically, they argued that school policy had, until Tony's arrival, been determined by faculty consensus, and now expectations for both faculty and the boys seemed to be handed down from the headmaster. One holder of this view was a highly regarded young biology teacher and football and wrestling coach, Bob Ryan. Ryan had been hired by Mayo-Smith and soon emerged as a central figure in the school as Dean of Students and was popular with the boys. Recognizing this, Tony thought they might be able to work together productively. But after months of tension between them and a series of written exchanges, Tony determined he and Ryan held incompatible views on how the school should operate and that it would be best if Ryan left the school. It was a hard reckoning for both men.

In the course of a Monday morning assembly, or Hall, Tony announced, among other things, that Mr. Ryan would be leaving the school at year's end, at which point Ryan rose from his seat in the hall, approached the stage, and asked if he could tell his account of why he would be leaving the school. He contradicted Tony's suggestion that they had mutually agreed that he should leave. He said he had been terminated for his belief that consensus and collaboration should direct school policy, not the imposition of authority. It was a wrenching moment for both faculty and the boys, and certainly a wrenching moment for Tony. The school was clearly at a crossroads, and the weeks ahead through graduation exercises were freighted with tension and uncertainty. What Tony's critics may not have understood is that he too treasured consensus, but not a consensus on what was at the moment most agreeable to all; the only consensus that mattered was a consensus about what was *right.*

When the following school year commenced in the fall, there were signs that the air had begun to clear. Eight new hires, including several who would become the faculty's defining figures in the decades ahead, replaced what had been the oppositional cohort during Tony's first two years. He sensed a gradual lightening of morale, and by spring a shared sense of purposefulness emerged that would define the school's signature trajectory for three decades. In the 1995 school history, *Schola Illustris*, published to commemorate the Roxbury Latin's 350th anniversary, Tony, who had spent a good deal of the previous seven years researching and composing the book, summarized what he believed to be the school's transformation under his leadership:

Roxbury Latin was founded as a classical school and it has, in all the best eras of its history, adhered to a classical curriculum. I believe that no curriculum is divinely ordained, but it seemed to me in 1974 — and it seems to me now — that our school should go with its traditional strengths. The classical curriculum has shown itself remarkably open to innovation and modification...Our departments today are hardly polishing tombstones. Each is always searching for better ways of "doing its thing" — and change is constant. We are rather like those owners of one of those temperamental British sports cars: we like the basic engine, but it needs constant and sensitive retuning. I believe that the basic engine of the classical curriculum — when finely tuned — is the best vehicle ever designed to teach a boy how to sort out information, how to read (in the broadest sense) with understanding, how to think with lucidity, and how to express himself with clarity.

"Rapidly Changing Times"

The Reverend Peter Gomes was not alone in opining that with respect to contemporary educational orthodoxy, Tony Jarvis did not "fit in." Tony himself was not troubled by this assessment. He saw little in prevailing educational thinking that he cared to fit in with. His school talks repeatedly rejected the notion that a school's mission should be to prepare students to adapt to and thrive in "rapidly changing times"—which he felt was equivalent to preparing students for the cultural trends of the moment, for *anything*. For Tony, the primary responsibility of educators is to invite students to a consideration of the values, achievements, and ideas—verities—that do not change over time. For Tony, the historical past was not a cautionary record of outmoded and constricting practices, but a revelation of the values and the kinds of human conduct that transcend particular cultural circumstances and contribute to fully realized lives. With respect to the historical record—the past—Tony stood by St. Paul's injunction "to hold fast to that which is good."

The habit of finding solace and inspiration in a better past may have been forged in the course of Tony's high school years at St. Mark's School in Southborough, Massachusetts. Tony grew up in Painesville, Ohio, a mid-sized town twenty-five miles east of Cleveland. In the post-war 1940s and '50s. Painesville was the kind of town portrayed in Norman Rockwell's magazine cover illustrations. Its downtown commercial buildings and tree lined neighborhood streets could have been the setting for Frank Capra's Bedford Falls in his classic mid-century film, *It's A Wonderful Life.* In his opening-of-term addresses to the boys Tony liked to draw on his early boyhood experiences in Painesville to illustrate various moral lessons. From his book, *Love and Prayers:*

...It was the summer of 1948. Shortly after my ninth birthday. We lived in a small midwestern town. Our street, Cadle Avenue, had perhaps fifty homes on it: sturdy, respectable middle-class two story six-room houses. Each house had a small front yard and a long back yard, but there was not much space between the houses. I could communicate with my best friend next door, from my window to his, in a low voice. Family squabbles in summer were always heard by the neighbors on either side.

In small-town America in those days there were no or-

ganized activities—no one went to summer camp, there was no swimming pool, no basketball court, no Little League, no television. We were left to our own devices from morning to night…

Having set the Painesville scene, Tony recounts a personal lapse of judgment and its consequences. After a bout of imaginary World War II Nazi hunting with neighborhood friends, one of them dares Tony to crawl into an elderly neighbor's garden and pull up the vegetables. Without reflection, nine-year-old Tony takes the dare and, crawling on his stomach, makes his way through the bordering trellises into the garden. He is so preoccupied pulling up row after row of carrots, onions, and other vegetables, that he fails to notice the approach of the woman who planted the garden. Caught in the act, he is marched home by his neighbor who informs Tony's mother what he has done. Tony is sent up to his room to wait until his father comes home from work. Duly terrified, Tony hears his father enter the house and his mother's explanation of what transpired with their neighbor. Tony's father leaves the house to survey the ravaged garden, then confronts Tony in his room. "*Why did you do this*?" Tony can think of no reason, and says he was dared to by his friends. His father is not interested in the dare. He tells Tony that he alone tore up the garden. *Why?* Tony has no answer. Tony's father, now very angry, pronounces the punishment. First, Tony will empty his piggy bank and give all the proceeds to the wronged gardener. He will go to the woman's house immediately, apologize, and offer his services to repair and otherwise tend her garden for the duration of the summer. Tony does as he is told and returns home, foregoing the family supper. His account concludes:

At about 8:30 my father came up as always to hear my prayers. He sat as always at the foot of the bed. As always I rendered my prayers to God and my father. At the end there was a short silence—which I, pathetic and pitiable, broke by saying, "I'm sorry, Daddy." "I know," he said, and he ran his fingers through my hair. And then he arose and returned down the stairs.

…And the power of a tiny gesture—his fingers through my hair. Despite my crime, I was not only understood, I was loved.

Tony offered this particular reflection to illustrate the salutary effects of genuine contrition and forgiveness. Like many of his talks to the school—and many of his sermons—a personal anecdote introduces a consideration of a larger moral or spiritual concern. Whether reading or hearing these anecdotes, one senses in the telling an intentional artifice: the events narrated are plausible enough, but in their simplicity and directness they convey something closer to fable than strictly observed reality. In both tone and structure, Tony's account of his boyhood vandalism of a neighbor's garden is not far from Beatrix Potter's *Tale of Peter Rabbit*. Moreover, the simplicity of the parable strikes a deeper and more resonant chord in the boys he addresses than would a more discursive argument for some improving quality or outcome. This particular anecdote also reveals something of the vulnerability of the nine-year-old Tony, as well as the tenderness with which the mature Tony regards his younger self.

Tony was fourteen, not nine, when he boarded the train at the Painesville station that would take him overnight to the boarding school to which he had been admitted, St. Mark's School in Southborough, Massachusetts. There was no tradition, even among more comfortably off families of Painesville, of removing children from the city's public schools and enrolling them in private schools, and certainly not to boarding schools in New England. Both Tony's mother and father, neither of whom had grown up in Ohio, were convinced that their boarding school experiences had deepened and broadened their outlook on the larger world.

The boy boarding the train to Massachusetts, while rangier and scholastically more accomplished than the garden invader described above, was not emotionally well armored to face the challenges and adjustments that would be required of him at his new school. Founded in 1865, St. Mark's School in 1953 still bore some of the signature features that had made it a favored preserve of Boston and New York elites. A fixture in what for years had been called the St. Grottlesex complex of New England boarding schools (St. Mark's, St. George's, St. Paul's, Groton, and Middlesex), St. Mark's was founded on the model of established British schools. As such, boys proceeded through what in Painesville would have been their freshman through senior years of high school in a graduated sequence of numbered Forms. St. Mark's went so far as to incorporate Eton College's game of fives, a kind of handball, into its athletic program. For decades prior to Tony's arrival, prominent families could "put down" (register) their sons at birth for eventual admission to St. Mark's. By the time Tony was admitted, the school had progressed to a more merit-based admissions process, but there remained a lingering aura of class and privilege. A character in F. Scott Fitzgerald's debut novel, *This Side of Paradise,* refers to St. Mark's as a prep school for the sons of "Boston Brahmins and New York Knickerbockers." One such brahmin, Francis Parkman, a 1915 St. Mark's graduate who left the Harvard faculty in 1930 to head St. Mark's for twelve years managed to recruit Pulitzer Prize winning poet Richard Eberhart to teach in the school's English Department as well as, briefly, W. H. Auden. Auden would write to a friend that St. Mark's "sets out to be a sort of American Eton." Graduates of the Parkman era include the likes of poet Robert Lowell and *Washington Post* editor Ben Bradlee.

But before the rarefied ethos of the school could begin to register to Tony, he was overwhelmed by the imposing mass of the schoolhouse. Completed in the 1890s, all of St. Mark's School—dormitories, classrooms, laboratories, chapel, gymnasium and dining hall—was housed under the single roof of an imposing four-story gabled brick and Tudor pile. On the ground floor level, open-air cloistered walkways connected classrooms to the school's other facilities. In all, the school in its cavernous complexity suggested at once a grand country estate and a vast monastery.

Surrounded by 250 acres of forest and meadow, the St. Mark's campus was unlike anything Tony had ever seen. In the course of his four years' residence, he would come to treasure the school's distinctive architectural feel and would forever afterward link the architectural power of the schools and churches he attended and served to the quality of his experience inside them.

As he progressed through the school's required course of study, Tony became a disciplined and productive student, productive enough to win admission to Harvard. Respectful of what the school asked of him, he was not notably happy there. Like most new boys, he was profoundly homesick, but unlike most of his fellow sufferers, the distance and difference from the world he had left in Painesville was almost too great to assimilate. St. Mark's drew its students primarily from New England. Its headmaster while Tony was there, William Wyatt Barber, had begun to build a more economically diverse student body, but most of the boys Tony came to know were wealthier, more widely traveled, and otherwise more worldly-wise than he was. Tony never told me that he felt disliked at St. Mark's, but he did tell me he felt lonely and unto-himself. The athletic program of the school was strong in the 1950s, and participation in competitive sports was required of all students. Athletic distinction was the surest route to popularity and acceptance. Tony was not athletic, though willing enough to try. He had almost no experience of team sports in Painesville. Years later, when addressing Roxbury Latin boys on the life lessons to be learned from failure and set-backs, he would refer to being cut from his school's teams or, when he was on one, riding the bench.

From what Tony told me about his school days, I got the sense that he sublimated his initial all-being Lost-ness into a lifelong embrace of three things that felt essential to St. Mark's. The first was the school's atmospheric Englishness. The founding headmaster, Joseph Burnett, set out to create a version of the great English boarding schools: Eton, Harrow, Rugby, Winchester. His model for doing so was St. Paul's School in Concord, New Hampshire, which had been founded ten years earlier for that express purpose and in which Burnett had enrolled one of his sons. St. Paul's was set up as an intentional departure from leading New England Academies like Andover and Exeter. Like St. Paul's, St. Mark's would incorporate the protocols and as much of the "muscular Christianity" ethos of the leading British schools as it could, though it stopped short of offering a cricket program, as St. Paul's did.

As a lonely and isolated new boy, Tony realized that being a middle-American Ohioan not only carried no cachet in this new setting, it was an occasion for ridicule, school boys being school boys. In time Tony came to understand that East Coast Americans who assumed a class and cultural superiority over Midwesterners felt in equal measure socially inferior to the British. In this realization, I believe, Tony's lifelong Anglophilia was, if not born, confirmed. Feeding his early leaning to all things British was the school library's substantial collection of English history books. Tony told me what "saved him" at St. Mark's was finding quiet places to read books about England.

What would in time be a more powerful influence on Tony than the school's British history collection was its chapel program. St. Mark's, like most of the other schools in the St. Grottlesex constellation, was an Anglican/Episcopal foundation. In the mid-1950's while Tony was there, daily attendance at chapel services was required, as were courses in sacred studies. In the decade to follow, a more diverse student body, including more non-Christians, required a shift to a more ecumenical, less sectarian focus. But for Tony St. Mark's was rigorously Episcopalian, which, among other things, offered some continuity with his prior life. He had been prayerful as a younger boy, and he was prayerful at St. Mark's. Along with selected classmates, he served the St. Mark's chapel as an acolyte, student warden, and occasional reader at services. For Tony, scholastic and spiritual considerations would be forever fused.

Except to tell me about how he was able to assuage his loneliness at St. Mark's by solitary reading, Tony rarely mentioned his experiences at school. I recall no fond memories of friends or favorite teachers. About his time at Harvard, he said almost nothing. The one event from his undergraduate years he referred to several times in the course of our friendship was not related to Harvard. He attended Sunday services regularly when he was in college, and drawn by what he had been reading about the life of Phillips Brooks, the famous nineteenth century rector of Trinity Church in Boston, he decided one Sunday to attend a service there. The sermon he heard, he said, convinced him to become a priest. Tony described it as a call to put aside immediate preoccupations and take stock of what you are living for. Tony heard it as a call to service. He didn't say "heroic" service, but I think that's what, at age twenty, he had in mind. Up through his seminary training and ordination, he pictured himself as a missionary in India.

While he was at Harvard Tony's Anglophilia found a satisfying outlet as he began, with very few dollars to spare beyond his living expenses, collecting autographs, letters, and photographs relating to the British royal family and their continental relatives. His sleuthing led him to Goodspeed's antiquarian bookstore on Beacon Street in Boston where he would make periodic purchases until the store closed its doors in 1996. Queen Elizabeth II was crowned the summer before Tony entered St. Mark's, and the televised pageantry made a deep impression. In subsequent years he augmented his collection of paper documents with trinkets—cups and saucers, glassware, ash trays—issued to commemorate the nineteenth and twentieth century coronations of British royals. At Cambridge, the weeks-long breaks between the three scholastic terms provided opportunities for Tony to take a train into London and hunt for similar treasures in the bookstores and antique stores dotting the streets surrounding the British Museum.

I was not above kidding Tony about his Anglophile leanings. I remember once asking him in fun if he favored the restoration of monarchies all over the world and being surprised by the vehemence of his denial before he realized I was joking. Occasionally we would browse through Goodspeed's together and, once, when we were in London at the same time, a wonderful shop he knew about in Russell Square that sold engraved views of Oxford and Cambridge Colleges and of England's great public schools. A few of his purchases were hung in his Cleveland apartment when we taught together and then in the headmaster's residence at Roxbury Latin, but I did not see the full extent of his collection until he put it on display in his Dorchester condominium after his retirement. The framed letters, autographs, and documents were closely hung and filled all the available wall space in his sitting room. The commemorative artifacts were displayed in three floor-to-ceiling glass fronted corner cabinets illuminated from within. The effect was visually stunning. If asked, but not otherwise, he would happily recount where, when, and for what little cost he had acquired each item. Besides making an impressive visual display, Tony's collection had over time become valuable. Appraised at 1.8 million dollars at his death, he bequeathed all of it to Eton College's Museum collection.

Already a pronounced Anglophile, Tony unsurprisingly chose to begin his graduate studies at Cambridge. In the early 1960s and still today very few American college graduates matriculate to either Oxford or Cambridge, chiefly due to structural differences in their programs. Unlike American liberal arts colleges and universities that require students to take a variety of courses in the arts, sciences, social sciences, and humanities, Cambridge undergraduates choose a field of study—physics, history, English literature—at the outset and study that exclusively. As a result, a Cambridge undergraduate completing a degree is generally more deeply grounded in subject matter than his American counterpart. Americans who, like Tony, enter Cambridge with a Bachelor of Arts degree, whether from Harvard or any other American University, enroll in what is in effect Cambridge's undergraduate program, which they will complete in two years. My impression is that Tony valued his time at Cambridge, but I think more for the history and splendor of the place than for any personal relationships he established there.

I can recall only three things Tony told me about his time at St. John's College, Cambridge. The first was an especially stirring sermon preached by the divinity scholar James Stanley Bezzant, who proposed that "every man knocking on the door of a brothel in Marrakech is looking for God." The second was an address to Cambridge's divinity faculty and students by American evangelist Billy Graham. As Tony recounted it, after acknowledging the depth of the Cambridge faculty and clergy's theological knowledge, Graham paused and asked his hosts, "How many of you have brought somebody to Jesus Christ today?"

The third Cambridge memory, to which he referred a number of times over the years, was of a damp, cold Christmas recess when, unable to afford to fly home, he arranged to meet up with his sister's Painesville boyfriend and later husband, Craig Smith, who was studying church music in London. The plan was to spend the holiday break together visiting cathedrals. On Christmas day Craig arrived in Cambridge in time for the two of them to attend the nationally broadcast King's College service of lessons and carols, after which they returned to London in time to attend midnight Mass at All Saints, Margaret Street. Tony confided to me that he was in tears for a good part of the day, the haunting beauty of the services somehow amplifying his longing for home and family. When I wrote to Craig Smith to check the accuracy of my recollection of what Tony told me, Craig confirmed the details, with one exception. In Tony's account, "*we* cried" for most of that day, though Craig could not recall crying in Tony's presence, but acknowledged there may have been some solitary tears due to missing Tony's sister, Faith. In all, Tony's confession of a tearful collapse while attempting to ease his home sickness by immersing himself in the English past seems continuous with his earlier efforts to keep his emotional balance while homesick at St. Mark's.

Several years after Tony and I had retired from our respective headmasterships, we flew together to attend to a summer conference of the International Boys Schools Coalition in Cape Town, South Africa. We decided to break up the journey with a three-day stop in London to take in some West End shows and stretch our legs sightseeing. On the second day I proposed that we take a train up to Cambridge and revisit our old college haunts. Tony agreed, and we had a long, pleasing high summer day of it. I led Tony through an erratic tour of my favorite pubs, the terraced house St. John's College provided for married students where my wife and I lived for practically nothing, the flat where my tutor in theology, W. Norman Pittenger lived. I recounted the night of the St. John's May Ball when, after my wife and I and our friends had danced for hours under the stars, bag pipers strode up to the battlements of the college's New Court just as dawn broke over the college gardens. I remember talking quite a lot about various people my wife and I had befriended or who had otherwise impressed me while I was there. Over lunch I asked Tony if there was any place he would like to revisit. None came to mind, but he did lead me to three or four college chapels where he spoke impressively about their architectural features and recent renovations, but not a word about memorable people or events.

Reticent as Tony was to talk about his life while in school, he was from the outset of our friendship intensely interested in mine. I believe he considered my educational trajectory to be his road not taken. I grew up in Arlington Heights, Illinois, a suburb northwest of Chicago. Arlington Heights families enrolled their children either in its public schools or in Catholic parochial schools. Until I read about them in books as a teenager, I was unaware that private schools—Prep Schools—existed, though a neighbor of mine who had some early scrapes with the police was sent away to a military academy in Indiana. My elementary school, junior high, and high school were all a short walk from my house. Arlington High School enrolled nearly three thousand students when I attended. Despite its size, I did not feel daunted as I proceeded through its scholastic and extracurricular programs alongside boys and girls I had known since elementary school. Several of those friendships went deep and have continued into my old age. There were also compelling, if sometimes distracting, amorous relationships. By my own subjective assessment, I was a fairly good student. My grades were mostly A's and B's, and I was actively involved in the school's choral groups, drama program, school newspaper, and athletic teams. Tony was fascinated by all of this and I believe envied it.

About my undergraduate experience at Middlebury College, he was even more curious. Mainly due to books I had read in high school, I decided that I wanted to go East to school. It was not a clearly worked out plan. I remember feeling that by going East, I might meet and mingle with the kind of people I had encountered in *Catcher in the Rye* and *A Separate Peace.* I especially hoped I would meet someone like Holden Caulfield. Moreover, I *did* meet a number of characters that seemed to come from that world. About half of my fellow freshmen at Middlebury were from Prep Schools. Unlike Tony, I never experienced homesickness going away to school. On arrival in Middlebury, my love of the place felt something like the love of a person. Ably and warmly reared as I had been at home in Arlington Heights, I never wanted to leave Middlebury, even for holidays, and given the expense and complications of travel back to Chicago, I rarely went home. Tony wanted to hear about all of this: the intellectual lights that tentatively blinked into being, my friendships and loves, including in my junior year love of a newly arrived freshman who would become my wife.

I wondered at first whether Tony's interest in my Middlebury experience might be his way of being courteous, especially given what I regarded as his own more gilded scholastic past. But over time it was clear. The idea of my being thoroughly and happily immersed in school resonated deeply with him. Middlebury College, or at least what I had recounted of it, became for Tony a good dream. The first faculty appointment he made as Headmaster of Roxbury Latin was negotiated over the summer before his first term at the school. On my recommendation, he hired a Middlebury friend of mine who was working in the Dean's office at the college. My friend was not at all sure he was qualified to be chairman of the English Department, as all of his prospective colleagues in the department seemed more experienced than he was, but such was Tony's elevated regard for Middlebury. That regard did not diminish through the years, and in a way he could not have imagined, it was rewarded.

At mid-career one of Tony's proudest hires was a confident, well-spoken Middlebury graduate, Michael Obel-Omia, who rose quickly through the Roxbury Latin teaching ranks to become Dean of Students and then

Director of Admission before, with Tony's blessing, moving on to the Upper School Directorship of University School in Cleveland. In his sixteen years working for Tony, Michael, an African American, had become one of the school's defining fixtures on the faculty. He had also, as an undergraduate, been focal enough that he was asked to serve as an alumni member of Middlebury College's board of trustees. As a trustee he was invited to nominate a candidate for an honorary degree, and he nominated Tony, who was about to commence his 30th and final year as headmaster of Roxbury Latin. The board confirmed Michael's nomination, and in the synchronous way of milestones in Tony's and my lives, my youngest daughter was to graduate from Middlebury in the ceremony in which Tony was honored.

Graduation day, it turned out, was unseasonably chilly with intermittent rain, and there were complicated logistics for getting the graduates, faculty, and staff lined up for their procession to the outdoor amphitheater where the ceremony would commence. I remember a mounting gladness as I made my way over muddy lawns to greet Tony in the standing line of gowned dignitaries waiting to process. I had to wait a few minutes to signal his attention, because he was in deep conversation with fellow honoree Meryl Streep.

I have no recollection of what we said to one another, but I think we both realized something we shared had come full circle.

Middlebury College was not the only institution of higher education to recognize Tony's distinctive contribution to the American educational complex. Six years earlier Bowdoin awarded him an honorary doctorate in humane letters. In 2018, Berkeley Divinity at Yale, in recognition of the program he established for those who felt called to Christian service in schools, awarded him an honorary doctorate in divinity. What I find striking in the conferring of these honors on Tony is that he was by no means a standard bearer for the educational mission espoused by elite and temperamentally secular colleges like Bowdoin, Middlebury, and Yale. Tony, by contrast, was deeply culturally conservative. Along with enlightened schools and colleges in the late twentieth and early twenty-first centuries, he embraced racial equality and diversity—but only in service of a higher good: schooling students to a reckoning with what composes a spiritually satisfying life. He invited that reckoning in nearly every talk he gave to the assembled boys and faculty of Roxbury Latin and in nearly every sermon he preached in the 50 years since his ordination.

The man honored by the likes of Bowdoin, Middlebury, and Yale chose to invest most of his working years in a small and circumscribed world. Roxbury Latin enrolled only 300 boys. Prior to Tony's arrival the school was venerable, but faltering. It had, through a combination of inertia and pride in tradition, maintained long-standing requirements in classical languages. While sons from prominent Boston families had enrolled their sons in Roxbury Latin over the years, that stream had dried to a negligible trickle by the time Tony arrived in 1974. At that time, apart from its most loyal alumni, Roxbury Latin was not considered an especially strong alternative to bigger, more progressive rivals, such as Milton Academy or Noble and Greenough. Unlike more prominent private day schools and the established New England Boarding Schools—Exeter, Andover, Groton, Deerfield, St. Paul's—Roxbury Latin was largely unknown outside of Boston. Neither I nor any of my colleagues at University School had heard of it until Tony left us to go there.

Tony's now widely acknowledged transformation of Roxbury Latin did not introduce a new curriculum or restructure faculty-student relationships to accommodate "rapidly changing times." Instead, he located what he believed had been the core excellence of the school over the centuries and, as he put it in *Schola Illustris,* tinkered with the engine. In doing so, he stood firm against the heady educational reforms that were reorienting independent schools in the 1970s and beyond. Besides standing by classical languages, Tony resisted going coed. A good deal of Tony's and my talk about schools over the years was about how boys thrive, or don't thrive, in school. We agreed, because we had both seen it, were both immersed in it, that boys are able to be fully themselves in a humanely conceived boys' school.

Tony also resisted arguments that increasing enrollment would provide revenue necessary to support everything from better plant maintenance to student financial assistance to faculty salaries. As stated in the Roxbury Latin prospectus Tony composed after his arrival, the school's central mission was to create a climate in which "every boy is known and loved." For love to have its transformative effect, the boys must first be known. "The single most important variable in this school," Tony liked to say, "it that it is small."

The progressive ideas which had come into play under Richmond Mayo-Smith's leadership were driven by a concern that traditional scholastic practices had petrified to the point of lifelessness. For many school leaders and school boards, failure to adopt reforms posed by the likes of Jonathan Kozol, Neil Postman, Paul Goodman, and others was to risk missing the educational boat. Tony saw no such risk, because a boat sailing off with a cargo of current educational nostrums was not for him a compelling metaphor. Throughout his adult life Tony's most withering personal criticism of anyone—politician, school head, journalist—was to say he/she "looks to see which way the wind is blowing" before committing to a course of action. For Tony, to sail with the wind was to sail blind. Moreover, with respect to educational practice, topical winds have a way of shifting, even reversing direction. In the decades to follow, perceived excesses of various school reforms of the 1960s and '70s generated radical correctives, including Back to Basics and Cultural Literacy movements. In 1979, ten years after co-authoring *Teaching as a Subversive Activity*, Neil Postman published a revised take on effective schooling, *Teaching as a Conserving Activity*.

For Tony, to conclude that the world is indeed rapidly changing requires a fixed perspective outside of that world. He had found that perspective in the course of his schooling, especially in his preparation for the priesthood. Throughout his teaching and preaching life the metaphor he would oppose to the bandwagon or missed boat was "city on a hill," Jesus's evocation in the Sermon on the Mount of a place above and apart from earthly vicissitudes. Because the city on a hill is elevated above its surroundings, its light is a steadying beacon. En route to the New World to found the Massachusetts Bay Colony in 1630, Puritan dissident John Winthrop preached to his fellow shipmates that the polity they were about to establish would be "a city on the hill," a light to the larger world. A few years later, another ardent Puritan, John Eliot, would arrive in Massachusetts Bay where he would found the Roxbury Latin School to serve the children of Winthrop's now burgeoning city on a hill.

Another earthly city on a hill favored by Tony was the monastic abbey established in the 6th century on the Scottish island of Iona. Art historian Kenneth Clark in his popular BBC television series, *Civilization,* opines that in the centuries immediately following the breakdown of Roman order in Europe, the shared culture that defines civilization had been splintered and lost. The closest thing to a unifying cultural thread were the remnants of Christian practice, but Christianity was no longer ascendant in the early centuries of the Middle Ages. A desperate monk, Columba, led a few followers to the remote and barren island Iona off the western coast of Scotland where they erected a monastery from the island's stone and wattle. Temporarily safe from the tribal ravages on the mainland and continental Europe, the monks of Iona celebrated Christian mass in the precise order and in the same Latin that had been in use since the Roman Empire's conversion to Christianity in the fourth century. From Clark's perspective, when all of civilization's lights had seemingly gone out in Europe, the monks of Iona resolutely carried on the sacred practices of an earlier, better age. Tony loved this story. For him Iona was a city on a hill, and a city on a hill was his unapologetic vision for Roxbury Latin.

THE LENGTH
AND SHADOW
OF TONY JARVIS

*"An institution is the length
and shadow of one man."*

—Ralph Waldo Emerson, *Self Reliance*

S chools are collaborative efforts, to which it might be added that schools succeed as collaboration succeeds. Crucial to effective collaboration is leadership. By any measure, Tony Jarvis was an effective leader of Roxbury Latin School over the course of his thirty-year tenure, but his approach to leadership drew on almost nothing from contemporary education theory or practice.

For most of the years (1974-2004) Tony led Roxbury Latin, the average tenure of American independent school heads was five and a half years, a span of time unlikely to contain what constituents might consider any kind of a Golden Age. In many instances, the five to seven year tenure of a school head describes an arc of failure: a new head arrives amid certain expectations; after a year or two there is schoolwide feeling that those expectations are not being met; trustees set criteria the head must meet in order to remain; after a year or two, it is determined there has been insufficient improvement; the trustees thank the incumbent head for his or her service and set about searching for a new head.

A number of factors have contributed to increasingly rapid turnover in independent school leadership. The job has increased in the amount and complexities of its demands. For centuries "headmaster" meant head *teacher* (Latin *magister*). Traditionally, school heads rose from the ranks of teachers of proven competence. Traditionally, headmasters taught classes in their specialties as well as assuming the direction of the school overall. With the rise of mid-twentieth century management science, the traditional role of teacher/headmaster was challenged by the notion of headmaster as organizational *manager*, skilled in strategic planning, resource allocation, and fund raising. School heads as managers delegated responsibilities for a complex of sub-organizations: admissions, professional development, curriculum development, college placement, alumni relations, plant management, and financial development. The school head as manager was a comfortable notion to school trustees who were often themselves managers of prospering private enterprises. The idea of running a school "like a business" and locating the right "manager" made good sense to trustees familiar with business practice.

The rise of the corporate manager type—the CEO—in schools was accompanied by another mid-twentieth century development, an increased tendency for unhappy constituents to litigate, or to threaten to litigate, school complaints in court. School heads determined to part company with what they believed were unproductive or obstructive faculty and staff were challenged in court to demonstrate they were not discriminating against their colleagues' age or sex or preferred cultural stance. Legal action, sometimes successful, was initiated against school heads by families unhappy about their child's disciplinary treatment, academic performance, college guidance, or athletic coaching. As his twenty-five year tenure was drawing to a close in 1988, my own headmaster, Rowland McKinley, would often remark, "You know, a headmaster cannot goddamn *do* anything anymore." As the coming millennium approached, it was increasingly acknowledged that private school headmastership had lost a good deal of *majeste.* The world of headmasters who set a distinctive and personal tone in their schools and schools that, in Emerson's phrase, were the length and shadow of their leaders—Peabody of Groton, Boyden of Deerfield—had become hard to imagine.

Except at The Roxbury Latin School. Consistently throughout his tenure Tony emphasized that the school's smallness was its chief virtue. Moreover, he knew himself well enough to know that he could personally manage a school of fewer than 300 boys. His initial assessment of the school's program in 1974 was that it was venerable and serviceable, and that assessment was only strengthened in the years to follow. As independent schools across the country rushed to incorporate new programs believed to be worthy—AIDS education, non-western history, non-western languages—they were forced to contend with new administrative complexities and costs. Nearly every school of my acquaintance acknowledged the allure of promising new programs, but also the difficulty, and sometimes impossibility, of eliminating old ones. From the outset Tony let it be known to his trustees, to his faculty, and to Roxbury Latin families that the school was committed to the depth of its program, not its breadth. When asked by parents on a number of occasions why the school did not offer Spanish, the most widely spoken language in the hemisphere, Tony answered "because we offer French and Latin and Greek."

Tony liked to proclaim "I know nothing about administration," a rhetorical stance that pleased him, but his personal oversight and direction of every aspect of the school's program—classroom instruction, discipline and guidance, admissions, college placement, plant services, fundraising, and faculty recruitment—became the defining feature of his leadership. His office was situated on the central concourse of the school near the entrance. His door was usually open when he was inside, and he was emphatically "available" to students and colleagues, occasionally more available than some of them may have preferred. One of his first faculty hires, a friend of mine, was both impressed and a little alarmed that if a particular class had not gone well that day, Tony seemed aware of it within minutes and would seek him out to inquire if everything was all right.

That Tony was able to be demanding of his colleagues but for the most part not oppressive was due, I believe, to a quality he had revealed when we were colleagues at University School: he never asked more of other faculty than he was willing to do himself. He continued to teach classes, both Western Civilization, a close version of the course we developed together in Cleveland, and English electives. In his later years, he did not teach his own Western Civilization class but would teach discrete units in areas of special expertise—medieval and renaissance art and architecture—to all the Western Civilization sections. Like the rest of his colleagues, he took on his share of student advisees. For years he composed the school's schedule and assigned the courses for each boy. He oversaw the meetings in which the admission of new boys was determined. He either composed or personally approved the school's official letter of recommendation for graduating seniors to their favored colleges. The coaches of Roxbury Latin athletic teams came to appreciate that Tony attended—and did not merely make an appearance—at their games and meets and matches. Tony did not miss a student play or concert. At the start of the school year, he would invite new boys and groups of returning students to casual receptions at his house. He had determined that the senior prom dance would be held at the school and that afterward he would greet the boys and their dates at a candle-lit reception at his house, a gesture in equal parts gracious and cautionary, given the era's prevailing expectations of prom night behavior.

One year, uncharacteristically and to his great annoyance, Tony was called out of town on prom night which meant he would be unable to meet and greet the seniors in the traditional way he had established. His seasoned faculty deputy, Mike Pojman, was entrusted with hosting the post-prom reception. Mike's account of the instructions left for him give some indication of the obsessive care Tony was inclined to take in such matters. In a celebratory talk Mike delivered on the occasion of Tony's twenty-fifth year as headmaster, Mike recited the list of instructions he had saved from the prom night in question:

Directions for hosting post-prom reception at my house:
- **Make sure punch bowls are set up properly in the dining room, one at each end table.**
- **There are to be no electric lights in the dining room, but don't light the candles too soon and don't light the candles and leave the house!**
- **You are to greet the guests as they arrive, not as they leave.**
- **There are to be no electric lights in the hallway, only candles. Don't light them too soon and don't light the candles and leave the house.**
- **Make sure you greet the guests as they arrive.**

— Open windows in the living room and in the dining room.
— Go up to my house just as the prom ends so you can greet the guests as they get to the house.
— There are to be no electric lights in the dining room or in the hallway. Only candles. But don't light them too soon (and don't light them and leave the house).

This was of course offered in affectionate fun for the assembled revelers. Mike Pojman was Tony's assistant headmaster and long-time faculty confidant. In the twenty years since he joined the Roxbury Latin faculty to teach chemistry and math, he had become a beloved fixture in the school. No one was in a better position to summarize to the assembled guests the impact of Tony's presence: "For the past twenty-five years Roxbury Latin has been 'Tony's Place.' He defines and embodies the classic Head Master—the lead teacher—the central figure in the daily life of the school. Certainly all who work with him feel 'the hand of Jarvis' in all aspects of the school's being."

That after a quarter century the school had come to feel to its constituents like "Tony's Place" was true of more than the school's general ethos. Tony also reconceived the physical campus. Throughout his own schooling, beginning with his arrival at St. Mark's, physical place mattered. He read deeply in ecclesiastical and scholastic architecture, and he had formed clear, highly particular preferences. A not insignificant factor in his decision to come to Roxbury Latin was his admiration of its school house, designed by William G. Perry in 1924 as the school prepared to move to its present location in West Roxbury. Perry's specialty was the restoration of historically distinctive buildings, and the gabled and turreted structure he proposed to the Roxbury Latin trustees featured both classical and Palladian touches. The historic signatures of the design helped to win Perry a thirty-year contract to design and restore buildings in Colonial Williamsburg.

In 1975 Tony invited me to read my poems in a morning Hall. I was eager to see his new school, and I was a little surprised by what I saw. My first impression as I approached the campus along busy Centre Street was of a closely settled strip of retail shops and modest frame houses. Turning uphill onto St. Theresa Avenue the school grounds appear on the right behind a substantial wrought iron fence. Once inside the school entrance, any sense of the surrounding neighborhood instantly recedes. Through a combination of topography and landscaping the Roxbury Latin campus becomes abstracted entirely from its surroundings. True to Tony's description, the schoolhouse was distinctive and charming, but it was not, in 1975, in immaculate good repair. Walls needed paint. The stairwells and corridors were scuffed and dingy. When the school day was over, Tony wanted to show me what he described as a much-needed improvement in the facility and led me down to what had, I think, been a maintenance area in the basement. Per Tony's instruction, the pipes and ductwork overhead had been painted a matte black, and a carpet had been laid over the cement floor. Some tables and chairs had been placed along the walls. As Tony began telling me about the creation of what he felt was a badly needed lounge area for the older boys, his face fell. Some paper cups and candy wrappers were strewn over the table tops, and there was paper and other litter on the carpet. Tony was stricken. On the way back upstairs he hailed a maintenance worker and told him to be sure the lounge was thoroughly cleaned. I had rarely seen Tony in such a dark mood. I think he wanted to show me a more impressive school.

It did not take long before he would be able to do that. With each successive visit the school, I noted its progressive transformation into "Tony's Place." The re-hanging of the school's traditional portraits which had begun, along with some initial resistance, the summer of his arrival continued apace throughout his tenure. Tony commissioned New York portrait artist Richard Owen to paint what became a succession of seventeen oil portraits of long-serving trustees and faculty. Acoustic tiles, overhead fluorescent lighting, plastic chairs, and other signature features of interior design of the 1950s and '60s were replaced by materials continuous with William Perry's original plan for the building. Individual globed reading lamps on the library tables replaced harsh overhead lighting. What had originally impressed me as a "shabby genteel" look to the place was soon no longer shabby.

Set a few hundred yards behind the school and hidden behind a stand of pines is the headmaster's residence, a substantial timber and stucco house which had been part of the estate purchased to build the new school in 1924. Inside, a spacious center hallway opens under wide archways to a large living room on the right and a large formal dining room and kitchen to the left. An elegant central staircase leads up to a master suite, which includes a comfortable upstairs sitting room, bedroom, and dressing room. Down the hallway are smaller bedrooms, including what were formerly servant quarters. In all, a lot of house for Tony who, except for his substantial library of books, a series of framed vintage posters from the First World War, and a collection of Ackermann prints of Cambridge colleges, brought very little with him from his apartment in Cleveland. Aware that the house would have to be at least minimally furnished and with little money beyond the prospect of his new salary, Tony arranged with the trustees to borrow $10,000 to furnish the house.

With the help of one of his Cleveland parishioners, Rosamund Groves, who made herself available from her summer house on Cape Cod, Tony managed to furnish the downstairs rooms, though to my eye very austerely. As it happened, the $10,000 did not go very far, because of Mrs. Groves' insistence, with Tony's compliance, on purchasing genuine antiques. As a result, the dining room featured an ancient but elegant dining table and chairs, a sideboard, and a worn but venerable oriental carpet. The living room contained a circular occasional table, two matching settees, two or three upholstered chairs and, to me inexplicably, a highly polished but unplayably damaged grand piano. In his thirty years' residence in the house, there were no further augmentations. The downstairs rooms were brightly fenestrated, but there were no curtains. There were gleaming expanses of uncarpeted hardwood floor. My wife and I were guests in that house dozens of times over the years, and I never entered it without a fleeting impression that it was unoccupied. Like his Cleveland apartment, the new house conveyed something parsonic, even ascetic. Though he was otherwise the warmest and most generous of hosts, getting any kind of breakfast at Tony's was a challenge. Church or school duties invariably required him to be up and out of the house before we rose for the day. Making our way down to the cavernous kitchen, we would open the refrigerator to find its shelves empty, with perhaps the exception of a single English muffin curled into the back of a box not recently purchased. There were sometimes tea bags which we would brew in a sauce pan.

But however austere Tony's domestic choices, he had an altogether different and grander vision for The Roxbury Latin School. Having befriended architect William Buckingham, an All Saints, Ashmont, parishioner, Tony was delighted to learn that virtually alone among his contemporaries, Buckingham shared both his preference for classical architecture and his aversion to modernist departures from traditional forms. Between 1986 and 2002, Tony and Buckingham collaborated on six major additions to the campus, beginning with the

Gordon Wing, which would house what was at first a Refectory (Tony's preferred term for dining hall) and now a choral room, a Great Hall, or general-purpose meeting space, and a new library. The Gordon wing was designed to knit seamlessly to William Perry's 1924 design, as would the Smith Arts Center (1990), the Bauer Science Center (1996), the Gordon Field House (2000), and the Jarvis Refectory Building (2002) honoring Tony's long service to the school. Departing not at all from the look and feel of the Perry building, these commodious additions featured Palladian windows, arches and columns, as well as certain nods to American colonial and British school buildings Tony especially admired. Tony's vision and Buckingham's gift were such that with the completion of each new project, it was difficult to imagine that the new structure had not always been part of the campus.

Conceiving of and seeing through a desired building project, even of one's home, is heady business for anyone, but for Tony who since his boarding school days had been held in rapt enchantment by the architectural force of his surroundings, the serial expansion of Roxbury Latin put him into a kind of dream state. He attended to every design and construction detail, not just to the precise matching of new to old bricks, but even to matching new to old mortar. His passion for each project's coming to be proved infectious to the benefactors who supplied the funds. Remarkably, the millions necessary to undertake so much new construction were raised without the standard complexity of extended capital campaigns, lead gifts, and broad appeals for supporting funds. Tony was able to cultivate the support of single donors and families, most of them long-serving trustees of the school, for each project which would bear the donor's name. The pleasing sweep of the Roxbury Latin campus when Tony left it in 2004 quadrupled the architectural footprint of the original building, in all a spectacular flowering of the promise he saw in the tired but good bones of the schoolhouse he took charge of on his arrival.

For Tony, the continuity of classical forms visible everywhere in his renovated school was more than ornamental; it was elemental, a message in stone of what endured and what matters. No less elemental was the "Englishness" that had sustained him as a solitary reader in the St. Mark's School library. Tony's Roxbury Latin would not only include a Refectory and a Great Hall; its wrestling facility in the renovated Gym would become the *Palaistra*, after the chamber in which ancient Greek and Roman schoolboys had once wrestled.

As a result of determined correspondence on Tony's part with Buckingham Palace staff, official greetings from the Queen were read to the assembled school on its annual Founder's Day. Another school whose operation could be credibly traced back to mid-seventeenth century colonial roots might with reason proudly celebrate what in Roxbury Latin's case was a visionary founding by a historically significant Puritan divine, John Eliot, Apostle to the Indians. Tony wanted to go back a little farther: to Eliot's English boyhood and education at Cambridge University's Jesus College. Eliot's work in the new world was, for Tony, English work, and by an extension possible perhaps only for Tony, Roxbury Latin was an English foundation. For the most part, the faculty and boys of the school accepted their headmasters' ardent Anglophilia in good natured bemusement.

There was, for example, no serious objection when Tony commissioned the New York painter Irwin D. Hoffman to do a portrait of Charles I, "King and Martyr," brandishing an imagined charter of Roxbury Latin School. To colleagues who questioned such a fanciful rendering—there is no historical evidence for such a charter—Tony explained that it might have been *possible* that some kind of document could have been conveyed by the king to John Eliot. But even Tony must have known that the charter represented in the portrait and boldly headed "Roxbury Latin School" could not have been imagined during the reign of Charles I, since for centuries after the school's actual founding it was formally deeded as "The Grammar School in the Eastern Part of the Town of Roxbury." The designation "Roxbury Latin School" was not formally registered by the Commonwealth of Massachusetts until 1947. The portrait of Charles I holding the charter was on display for years in the school's central corridor and is now on view in the Jarvis Refectory.

Tony's attempt to ground the existence of Roxbury Latin in Englishness reached its apotheosis in 1992 as he began preparations to celebrate the school's 350th anniversary in 1995. To document that the school was indeed an English foundation, he made a case to the British Crown's College of Arms, established in 1484 by King Richard III, that since the school's first 138 years of existence were carried out under Massachusetts' allegiance to the British Crown, the school might be considered for a royally sanctioned coat of arms. That such a request was a long shot is confirmed by the fact that the coat of arms, duly conferred by the splendidly uniformed College of Arms' Garter King at a special school assembly, was the first royally approved emblem ever

granted to an institution outside the British Commonwealth. The coat of arms depicts Massachusetts' iconic
pine tree growing out of the open Bible John Eliot composed for the Algonquin Indians of the region. Flanking
the pine tree are the figures of Eliot in Puritan clerical
garb and the blind poet Homer, an image pictured for
years in the school's official seal. Overhead is a gilded
lion, rampant, wearing a gold crown signifying connection to Jesus College of Cambridge University, John
Eliot's alma mater. Spanning the bottom of the composition is a banner bearing the school motto: *Mortui vi-
vos docent* (the dead teach the living). For Tony historic
symbols, including heraldry, conveyed timeless lessons
to present observers. With the dedication of the new
coat of arms, the Englishness Tony treasured was now
forever burnished into the school's story.

Whether fascinated or amused by it, the constituents of the school, including the boys, were by no
means impervious to the headmaster's Anglophilia.
In ways that may have sometimes surprised them, the
school's ambient Englishness worked its way into old
fashioned school spirit. In Tony's early years as headmaster Roxbury Latin's athletic profile was relatively
modest among the New England schools composing
the Independent School League (ISL). At the time Tony

explained to me with some force that the reasons for this were obvious. First, Roxbury Latin enrolled the fewest boys in the high school grades of any of its rivals. Second, scholastic excellence and other essential school values were not going to be sacrificed on the altar of Winning. He confided to me that he actually liked the status of perpetual underdog, while acknowledging with some pride that, small enrollment aside, the school still turned out competitive wrestling and baseball teams. Big roster sports like football, Tony declared, were never going to carry Roxbury Latin to glory—until not too many years later they began to do it.

Among the hundreds of memorable athletic moments Tony witnessed from the sidelines and bleachers of Roxbury Latin's home and away contests, one stood out as emblematic of everything he had hoped for the school. In 2002, the Roxbury Latin football team finished its regular season undefeated and was scheduled to play a post season game against Rye Country Day School for the New England championship. Because of the distance between the schools, it was agreed that the game would be played on a neutral field on the campus of Avon Old Farms School in Connecticut. The game was scheduled for a Saturday, but there were complications. Seven of the Roxbury Latin starters were also performing in a production of Oliver Goldsmith's eighteenth-century comedy, *She Stoops to Conquer.* A normal afternoon kickoff would make it impossible for the actors on the team to get back to West Roxbury in time for their 8 p.m. curtain. Tony insisted that the game could not be played unless it started promptly at noon, to which the Rye coaches ultimately agreed.

That November Saturday was chilly with intermittent rain. Due no doubt to weather and the distance from home, only about thirty parents and other Rye supporters were on hand to cheer on their team. By contrast, more than 350 Roxbury Latin fans showed up, including most of the student body, many faculty, and alums from as far afield as New York City. They were not disappointed, as the Roxbury Latin eleven dominated the game, leading 20-0 at half time and winning 28-6. In the fourth quarter, when it was clear Roxbury Latin would be victorious, the boys on the sidelines burst into a rousing version of Hubert Parry's "Jerusalem," Headmaster Jarvis's favorite hymn and the choral work most certain to make him cry.

"Jerusalem" is a setting of a visionary poem by William Blake recounting the apocryphal legend of the youthful Jesus accompanying Joseph of Arimathea on a voyage to England:

And did these feet in ancient time,
Walk upon England's mountains green:
And was the holy Lamb of God,
On England's pastures seen!

One line of the poem references "chariots of fire," and the popular 1982 film of that title featured the hymn in its soundtrack. That year a rising star and choral director on the Roxbury Latin faculty, Kerry Brennan, asked Tony if he might introduce "Jerusalem" to the repertoire of songs and hymns the boys sang in assemblies. Never was a permission more gladly given, and that is how on a cold and rainy Saturday in Connecticut there would be a student body cheering on their football team to:

I will not cease from Mental Fight,
Nor shall my Sword sleep in my hand:
Till we have built Jerusalem,
In England's green & pleasant land.

Colleagues standing with Tony on the sidelines as the game ended agreed that they had never seen him happier.

STORIES AND SERMONS

_____

In the half century following his ordination and the commencement of his teaching life Tony addressed congregations, school assemblies, and other audiences thousands of times. Many of these addresses were delivered to his students at Roxbury Latin and his parishioners at All Saints, Ashmont in Dorchester, but there were hundreds of others, as by mid-career he had become a much sought-after guest preacher and guest speaker at schools, colleges, and educational conferences. Outside of the United States, Tony spoke and preached to audiences and congregations in Great Britain, Australia, New Zealand, South Africa, and Botswana.

I wasn't counting, but I believe I have heard Tony speak and preach fifty or sixty times, and in every instance he clearly moved his listeners, and he moved me. Even when I heard him give a talk which was a close version of one I had previously heard, the impact of the message was undiminished. Tony's manner at the pulpit or podium was in no way dramatic. He was serious, a bit reserved. His voice was clear and pleasing, the pace of his remarks unhurried. There were no rhetorical flourishes. When at my invitation he spoke at University School, I always asked for a copy of his remarks to include in school publications. The manuscripts he gave me were typed in narrow, widely spaced columns filling only half the width of the page. This he told me enabled his eyes to pass over the shortened lines in a way that reduced verbal stumbling.

Like other effective speakers I have known, Tony was always well-prepared. I never heard him depart from his written text, but there was little sign that he was reading one, as he seemed most of the time to be looking out into his audience. He took the same care with his manuscripts as he did with the organization of his extensive library; his talks were filed by theme, and he made careful records of the audiences addressed and the dates of each presentation. He was not reluctant to deliver a prior talk to a new audience if he felt the message was appropriate, and he sometimes combined elements of earlier talks. He was not concerned about repetition and assured the Yale Divinity students he taught after his retirement from Roxbury Latin that they should not be concerned about repeating essential themes in their sermons, as essential themes cannot be repeated enough; repetition helps to drive them home.

In thirty years Tony never delivered the same talk twice to the assembled boys and faculty of Roxbury Latin, but the same themes were central to all of them. Forty of his opening-of-term talks were collected in *Love and Prayers: A Headmaster Speaks to the Next Generation*, published in 2000. Tony ordered the selections by theme, not chronologically, and it was not surprising to me or to other readers I have talked to that the first talk to appear was "What Am I Doing Here?" I had heard the opening anecdote of this talk so many times over the years that I could not resist kidding Tony about it— along the lines of "Tony, have you ever come across a former student at a bus station or an airport who didn't report his failure discover the meaning of life?" I will not relay Tony's response, lest readers find it unbecoming of a clergyman. "What Am I Doing Here?" begins:

I was returning on the last train from downtown Boston, the 10:30 P.M. from South Station. Seconds after I sat down, a recent graduate of the school noticed me and came to join me. He's now in his early thirties. In his triumphal progress through the school and college and graduate school, he won all the glittering prizes. To his contemporaries, his meteoric rise in business defines the word "success."

Our conversation began with superficial chitchat—he

*lamenting that our train—the 10:30 P.M.!—"left so early,"
since he still had more work to finish at the office. Then his
tone changed, and he added, in a different voice, "You know,
ever since I was in school, almost all my days have been like
today—never enough time to do what I need to do. I worked
incredibly hard in school. I worked incredibly hard in college. I worked incredibly hard in business school. And now I
work incredibly hard at my job. Through school, college, and
graduate school I never really asked myself, "Why am I doing this?" I was always just focused on getting the next crucial credential. Every now and then, however, over the last
few years—for a few frightening moments—I have actually
stopped and asked myself, 'Why am I doing this? Why have I
chosen this life? Why am I working so hard?' As hard as I try
to repress these questions, they keep popping up."*

*By the time he finished this confession, the train was
nearing my stop and I was every so slightly daunted by the
task of disclosing the entire meaning and purpose of existence
in the remaining seventy seconds of my journey. For some
reason James Thurber flashed through my mind, and I asked
if he had ever read Thurber's short story, "The Sea and the
Shore." He hadn't, so I faxed it to him next morning and it
became the focus of our next conversation.*

*Thurber writes about the lemmings, the small rodents
that live on Scandinavia and are best known for their in-*

explicable periodic tendency to rush from the land to the sea—to certain death. In Thurber's story, one "single excited lemming" looks at the setting sun on the ocean and cries out, "Fire! The world is coming to an end!" as he rushes precipitously into the sea. Mass hysteria grips the other lemmings, and in tumultuous flight—amid rumors and panic—the other lemmings follow him headlong into the sea. As they drown, some shout, "We are saved!" while others cry out "We are lost!"

In case we miss it, Thurber tells us the moral of the story: "All men should strive to learn before they die what they are running from, to, and why."

Like so many of Tony's talks and sermons, this one begins with a personal anecdote. As in the anecdote cited earlier about his boyhood incursion into his neighbor's vegetable garden, there is something burnished and simplified in the telling, casting the central issue into the clearest possible relief. Life, even an outwardly successful life, begs at some point a reckoning with meaning and purpose; the unexamined life is *not* worth living. For Tony's readers and listeners, the factual veracity of the incident he has just recounted—*did* the oppressed high achiever he encountered on the train really, in minutes, begin to question the meaning of his life?—is beside the point. The incident succeeds as a fable, and in this instance Tony underscores the moral of the "real life" fable with something closer to Aesop: Thurber's fanciful story of the lemmings.

"What Am I Doing Here" is a fitting introduction to *Love and Prayers* because it asks the meaning question at the heart of all of Tony's preaching and teaching. Asking the meaning question, however, poses the daunting task of answering it. In readily accessible terms, Tony's answers follow the lineaments of Aquinas' argument for the existence of God: first, demonstrate what God is obviously not, then establish the necessity of filling the void. In terms the growing boys of his school could understand, Tony laid out what is ultimately not meaningful or satisfying in life, including the recurring allure of power, fame, and money: the "glittering prizes." Making the team, being star of the team, being top scholar, getting into the most selective college, being good-looking, wildly popular, accepted, "in"—in sum, everything a reasonable boy might assume would make him happy will ultimately fail to do so. Believing otherwise was a sure ticket to meeting Tony on a train and confessing existential emptiness. But if the glittering prizes do not deliver, what does?

If the central question in Tony's talks and sermons

was often simply posed, the solution was not. Tony did not address the meaning question with bromides; he proposed instead a consideration of hard realizations and hard choices. Addressing life's inevitable disappointments, disillusionment, and occasional despair, Tony liked to draw on writers and thinkers well qualified to report. In his response to the crisis of meaning raised in the "What Am I Doing Here" talk, Tony cites the classicist Frances McDonald Cornford's poem about the condition of outwardly gilded youth:

Magnificently unprepared
For the long littleness of life.

A minute later he quotes T.S. Eliot to demonstrate the emptiness of settling for that long littleness:

A cry from the North, from the West and from the South
Whence thousands travel daily to the timekept City…
And the wind shall say: Here were decent godless people
Their only monument the asphalt road
And a thousand lost golf balls.

Tony is aware that he is addressing, among others, thirteen-year-old boys, to whom he will not condescend.

He concludes with an invitation to live differently, an invitation extended every time he addressed the school:

There is another way. It is the way chosen by the few in every generation who are courageous enough to face the existential reality of their own mortality, of their own modest place in the universe. It is the way of the few who—fully aware of the smallness of their own lives—are somehow, nevertheless, empowered to use what little they have for causes and concerns beyond—and greater than—themselves. The way of the few is the harder, more lonely, more costly way. Someone asked Mother Teresa of Calcutta shortly before she died, "Why did you give up family and money and security to go and live among the destitute and hopeless?" In a flash, she replied, "I wanted a very hard life."

…Most of you already know that the only life worth living is the hard life. The hard life is the better way. Whatever else the harder way is, it is not dull. It is, I would submit, much more exciting, much more rewarding and, dare we say it, much more fun.

Whatever attendant fun the harder life might include Tony tended to leave to the boys' imaginations. In his talks in Hall, in his classes, and in his personal conversations with students, he insisted that even the youngest boys confront the most unsettling questions, including their own mortality. Tony opened another beginning-of-term talk with an anecdote about a visit to his grandparents in western New York state when he was ten. In the course of the visit, his grandparents took him along to console an old friend of theirs, a farmer, who had just lost his wife to illness. To Tony's surprise the departed woman was lying in state in a casket on the dining room table.

It was my first experience of death, the first time the finality, the bleakness of death had hit me. I was the only child there and I stood alone gazing out the kitchen window at the bleak landscape of death, the snow covered fields… "If people can just die," I said to myself, "What's the point of anything?" That stark question is one that I would bet most of you have at some point asked yourselves: "What is the point of it all?"

Tony's insistence that the boys of Roxbury Latin come to a reckoning with their own mortality extended beyond the relative safety of childhood memories. In an address titled "Attitude" Tony related his experience of the passing of a much beloved member of the student body.

Some years ago, Billy McDonald sat in the seats you now occupy. Captain-elect of football, he was diagnosed with leukemia at the end of his Class II year; he was seventeen years old. Chemotherapy that summer reduced his two hundred pound body by almost a hundred pounds; all of his hair fell out. At first he felt sorry for himself. Until he was seventeen, everything had gone well for him. A golden future had seemed to beckon. Now he was dying. Of course he felt self-pity.

Then one day his whole attitude changed. He went down to the cancer ward for little children and saw tots two, four, and six years old who, like him, were facing almost certain death from cancer. When I visited him that night, the first words he said were, "I guess I'm really lucky." "Why's that?" I asked. And he told me about visiting the little kids, and then said, "At least I've had seventeen years…"

From then on, Billy was no longer a victim. He could not change the cruel reality life had dished out to him; he knew he was going to die (and in fact he was dead by the following March, two months before he would have graduated). But… he did not become a "victim." He took control of his responses to life's realities. His attitude was…I will face all of this horror cheerfully and positively and with dignity. And he did.

Tony told the boys of Roxbury Latin, his parishioners at All Saints, Dorchester, and every other group of listeners he addressed the same thing: if you live long enough and are honest enough to take an objective measure of your circumstances, you are going to be brought up short by setbacks, if not outright failure. You are going to lose things: friends, beloved family, competitions, status, former abilities and attainments; ultimately, you will lose everything. This message is very possibly the last thing most people, including growing boys, want to hear. Tony not only insisted that they hear it, but also the healing, deepening transformation that occurs when one is able to suffer and carry on.

Tony concluded the selected addresses in *Love and Prayers* with a talk titled "Tough and Tender." In it he makes the case for redemptive suffering.

Life is tough and we are vulnerable. The real man does not run away from life; he is not afraid to admit his vulnerability.

One great benefit of admitting our own weaknesses and vulnerability is that in doing so we become aware of the weaknesses and vulnerability of others. Some years ago Mother Theresa spoke at the Harvard commencement. She looked out at the great sea of satisfied graduates on their way to success and glory, and she dared to offer them as her graduation present the poor and suffering of the world. She told of visiting a family in Portugal. The youngest child in this family was grotesquely deformed and hopelessly retarded. "What is his name? What do you call him?" she asked the mother. "We call him our Professor of Love, because he has taught us how to love."

This helpless child—whom many families would regard as a curse and a burden—was seen by this family as a blessing. In his helplessness he evoked the attention, the sympathy, and the affection of every member of the family. "We call him our Professor of Love, because he has taught us how to love."

Every failure, every defeat, every bit of suffering we experience (as we risk vulnerability by opening ourselves to others) makes us stronger...Our sufferings, our failures, our defeats can become for us professors of love: they make us sensitive to the burdens and sorrows that others must bear.

Redemptive suffering was central to Tony's teaching and preaching through the very end of his life. After his retirement from Roxbury Latin, Tony arranged through his friend Eric Anderson, formerly headmaster and then provost of Eton College, to serve for two years as college chaplain. It is hard to imagine a more restorative and more fitting posting for Tony after Roxbury Latin. Here his immersion in Englishness was complete. The Eton College Chapel in which he would preach, attend daily services, and listen to its world-renowned choir, is an architectural masterpiece, a twin of Cambridge's King's College Chapel, both established in the fifteenth century by King Henry VI. A young colleague of Tony's and now Eton housemaster, Mike Grenier, recalls Tony's presence at the school:

He was a brilliant teacher and tutor, looking after groups of boys with kindness and compassion. It may not come as a surprise, though, to know that he was occasionally taken aback by the moral relativism that affects Etonians more than the students of Roxbury Latin, and I vividly remember him reflecting on the ease with which Etonians attempted to be "economical with the truth" (a phrase famously used by an Old Etonian cabinet secretary in a court case in the 1980s). Tony was not easily hoodwinked…

He loved the richness of the boarding school day and especially the rich tapestry of music, drama, and evening talks. I think he loved returning to being a teacher with none of the burdens of leadership.

Tony told me that he did love these things, but given his class preparations, grading, counseling, and chaplaincy duties, he told me he worked harder at Eton than at any other time in his life.

In 2008 Tony was called by the Berkeley Divinity School at Yale to direct a new program in Educational Leadership (ELM) for students considering carrying out their spiritual vocations in schools. For seven years, until his cancer symptoms and treatment made it impossible to continue, Tony designed and taught the program's courses and personally guided ELM students along their progress to ordination or to non-clerical posts in schools across the country.

For each of those seven years, Tony invited me to the Divinity School in February to teach classes on either a novel of mine, *The Headmaster's Papers,* or *I Can Learn from You,* a study I completed with a co-researcher Michael Reichert about how teacher-student relationships affect scholastic and developmental outcomes. I enjoyed every one of these Yale visits. It was of course good to see and catch up with Tony, as always a generous host. It was also fascinating for me to see Tony at work with his new students, bright, serious men and women, ages ranging from early twenties through middle life. What struck me at once is that his classroom stance with them was *exactly* what it was with the ninth-grade boys we both taught at University School. He had clearly established warm personal relationships with all of them. Light, joshing banter was exchanged as they entered and left the classroom, but once class began, he got rigorously down to business, drawing out and challenging their responses to the assigned texts, encouraging argument, acknowledging insights. The classes I observed and participated in were between an hour and ninety minutes in length, and they were very much Tony-directed. He did not hesitate to be firm. In a tone I recalled from our work together a half century ago, Tony reminded students at the outset of a class that it was non-negotiable and *essential* that they come to class having read every word and every page of the assigned material. To do otherwise was insulting, and he recommended that anyone unprepared should skip the class and find a quiet place to do the reading instead.

The Berkeley Divinity School is an Episcopal subdivision of the more widely ecumenical Yale Divinity School. Students admitted to the ELM program meet daily for an early Morning Prayer service before classes and most of them attend an additional mid-morning all-Divinity School chapel.

Early arrivals at the Berkeley morning service would find Tony already present in the sanctuary, kneeling in prayer. This observation was conveyed to me by one of those early arrivers, Tyler Montgomery, a rangy young man who after a prodigious scholastic and athletic undergraduate career at Penn and a stint in the Peace Corps in Costa Rica, chose to resolve his own meaning questions in the ELM Program. Like many of his classmates, Tyler and Tony progressed from a rigorous mentoring relationship into a personal friendship. In the course of my guest appearances at the Divinity School, Tony included Tyler and other students in the dinners we shared at the conclusion of the academic day. Tyler is one of several of Tony's Yale students I have kept up with as well, and he has made it clear to me that Tony's example, teaching, and friendship have been as formative as anything else in his life. In acknowledgement Tyler invited Tony to Williamsburg, Virginia, to deliver the sermon on the occasion of his, Tyler's, ordination to the priesthood.

On that day in December of 2015, Tony had already received his terminal cancer diagnosis and had determined to resign his post in the Divinity School. The sermon he delivered managed not only to celebrate Tyler personally but also to honor the scriptural lesson assigned for the service: "And I heard the voice of the Lord saying, 'Whom shall I send, and who will go for us?' Then I said, 'Here I am! Send me." [Isaiah 6:8]

What Tony had to say to Tyler and to the congregation that day is exactly what he had to say to the boys of Roxbury Latin at the commencement of every new term.

Most people Tyler's age—the vast majority of people of all ages, in fact—just go with the pack…At Yale, for example, every June some 250 of the brightest and best seniors rush to Wall Street for phenomenal starting salaries. The elite group sees money, and they follow the pack—because without thinking much about it, they assume Wall Street equals success and that money equals happiness…

You, Tyler, have not followed the pack. You have actually looked at the big picture and asked the big question: "What do I want to do with my one and only earthly life? Where is happiness in life really found?" Unlike most people in every generation, you have listened and you have therefore heard the Still Small Voice of God actually calling you to something with your one and only earthly life, to do something great with your one and only earthly life…

You, Tyler, understand the great secret that undergirds the true Christian life. It is a secret that is right out in the open, but most people never see or hear it. That secret is best expressed by the author of the Epistle to the Hebrews who reminds us of the most obvious truth about human life: "Here on earth," he says, "we have no continuing city." We are not permanent residents of earth…Pierre Teilhard Chardin [wrote] "We are not human beings on a spiritual pilgrimage. We are spiritual beings on a human pilgrimage."

…I was ordained to the priesthood 50 years ago. Despite all the costliness of being a priest, I have had the happiest life of anyone I know. Every morning as a priest you get out of bed with the possibility that you might be able to help someone, that you might even be able to change someone's life for the better…

Tyler, you have heard the call to this vision of life, and you have responded: "Here I am. Send me."

On August 26, 2018, three weeks before he died, Tony preached his last sermon to the congregation of his beloved parish of 40 years, All Saints, Ashmont. A week earlier he had told me that his cancer had progressed to his brain, and while that had caused no pain or even discomfort, he found himself losing track of where he was in his thoughts and in his conversation, and he hated it.

There was no sign of impairment in the sermon, "Put Your Hand into the Hand of God," he delivered that morning. He began with a tribute to the long national service of Senator John McCain, whose life has been "heroically and sacrificially given to others."

There was no mention of the senator's own terminal brain cancer diagnosis.

Tony proceeded directly to the message he had imparted to the boys of Roxbury Latin in the opening talk of his *Love and Prayers* book. He cites again Frances Cornford's poem in remembrance of his Cambridge contemporary, Rupert Brooke, who fell ill and died while serving abroad in World War I:

> *A young Apollo golden-haired,*
> *standing on the brink of strife,*
> *magnificently unprepared*
> *for the long littleness of life.*

> *"The long littleness of life." Even the most brilliantly successful of our friends and contemporaries inevitably experience "the long littleness of life." They do sometimes experience moments of golden and rapturous insight, but such moments are inevitably followed by moments like what the disciples—and dare we say Jesus—experienced in today's Gospel—times of hopelessness and despair.*

Again in the spirit of his talks to the Roxbury Latin boys, Tony stresses the universality of feeling lost, of suffering. The redemptive way through suffering lay in reaching out to God, a message he hoped to bring home in the manner it was brought home to him when he was a lost and lonely schoolboy in the library quiet of St. Mark's—when something reassuring and English pointed the way.

I want to conclude this morning with a story I have told before. I remembered it again this past week when I was reading about the early days of World War II. The story became well known to me because King George made it the conclusion of his Christmas broadcast to all the nations of the British Empire at Christmas 1939 when England stood alone against the tyranny of Nazi Germany. Still today—in our time—the Sovereign's Christmas Day message is the most widely listened-to broadcast in the world. King George's 1939 Christmas message has words we need to remember as we face those moments of great discouragement in life:

"I said to the man who stood at the Gate of the Year: 'Give me a light that I may tread safely into the unknown.' And he replied, 'Go out into the darkness and put your hand into the hand of God. That shall be better than light and safer than a known way.'"

Parish and School

Kerry Brennan, who succeeded Tony as Roxbury Latin Headmaster in 2004, had an informed perspective when asked by *Boston Globe* obituary writer Bryan Marquard to assess Tony's achievement over his long tenure at the school. Kerry had been hired by Tony in 1978 to direct the school's music program in addition to other teaching and coaching duties. In the subsequent eight years Kerry emerged as a popular and admired fixture on the faculty before, with Tony's blessing, departing for Cleveland's University School to assume the Directorship of the Lower School, then the Directorship of the Upper School. Kerry and I worked together productively for fourteen years before he was called to be Headmaster of Collegiate School in New York City.

Through the intervening years, Kerry had, as I had, maintained and deepened his friendship with Tony. Such had been his experience at Roxbury Latin and such had been his regard for his old mentor that Kerry, though still newly established at Collegiate, offered his candidacy at Roxbury Latin. Standard protocol dictates that retiring headmasters stand aside from the selection of their successors, but nobody at Roxbury Latin doubted that Tony thought the appointment of Kerry to succeed him would be a godsend. In response to *The Globe's* inquiry, Kerry said, "Tony tended to the school as if it were his parish."

Tony himself often likened his relationship to the school to his relationship with his parishioners. From the onset of his working life in Cleveland, he had simultaneously served both school and parish—and somehow served them both full-time. I do not believe Tony could imagine carrying out his life otherwise. He was elated when the Bishop of Massachusetts assigned him to All Saints, Ashmont, a national architectural landmark and a church with a legendary founding.

Tony loved All Saints right down to the granite and limestone blocks that composed it. He also liked to tell the story of how it came to be. Originally a modest frame structure serving working class Episcopalians who lived in Dorchester along the Old Colony rail line, the church would be radically transformed in consequence of an unexpected visit to one of its services. In the winter of 1879 on the Feast of the Holy Innocents, Father Bennitt, then Rector of the church, preached an especially affecting sermon in which he referred to his recent loss of a beloved child. Bennitt was unaware that in the course of the service an unfamiliar couple had slipped into the back of the sanctuary. They were Colonel Oliver Peabody and Mary Lathrop Peabody, wealthy denizens of nearby Milton—and Unitarians!—who were halted in their progress to their own church by the sudden onset of a blizzard that made further progress in their carriage impossible. Their carriage driver, a parishioner of All Saints, suggested that they take shelter there.

As it happened, the Peabodys too had just lost an infant daughter, and Father Bennitt's sermon combined with the welcoming feel of the place, moved the Peabodys to attend again the following Sunday, after which the colonel made a sizeable offering to the parish poor. The Peabodys thereafter took instructions in the Episcopal Church, were confirmed, and went on to lead the parish to construct the Gothic Revival church that stands today. The architect selected for the job was twenty-six-year-old Ralph Adams Cram, and All Saints, now a designated national monument, was his first major commission. Cram would go on to design some of the most distinctive Gothic Revival structures of the twentieth century, including The United States

Military Academy at West Point, St. John the Divine and St. Thomas Cathedrals in New York City, The chapel and academic buildings of Princeton and Rice universities. To Tony, steeped in architectural history since his school days, to serve such a parish in such a place was providential.

That service was also providential for All Saints. Noting that the average tenure of an Episcopal rector is currently under five years, the present Rector of All Saints, Fr. Michael Godderz, considers Tony's 42 years' service to the church "astounding." Over those years Tony was more than a heavily contributing Priest Associate. As the longest serving cleric, he came to represent the church's institutional memory, and he was a critical factor in building a faltering congregation up to its current size of 350. For two years, between 1996 and 1998, Tony became acting Rector of the parish while an extended search was carried out that led to Fr. Godderz's appointment. While Tony assumed those new—and very much full-time—interim duties, he refused to accept compensation on the grounds that he was adequately paid by Roxbury Latin, and there were more immediate needs for those funds in the parish. Though I am sure Tony felt he was "adequately" compensated by the school, he had, by 1996, arranged with the trustees to cap his salary at an annual figure a little higher than the top faculty salary—hundreds of thousands of dollars less than the headmaster salaries of other leading New England private schools. "I am, after all, a priest," Tony would explain to people who asked.

Though the All Saints congregation was aware Tony was ill, his death in 2018 registered as a profound loss. Fr. Godderz paid his old friend the following tribute in a letter to the parish:

For All Saints' this has been a year of incredible change. We're a faith community which takes seriously the injunction to hold fast to what is good. We lovingly preserve and nurture a vibrant tradition of faith, the full Catholic faith in all the glory of its Anglican expression. Yet, of course, even we cannot escape change.

Preeminent amongst those changes is the death of our dear friend and priest associate, Fr. Tony Jarvis. In a day when the average Rector's tenure is under five years, Fr. Jarvis's forty-two years' service amongst us is astounding. And it was offered as gift to us while working full time, as Headmaster of Roxbury Latin School and later while teaching at Berkeley Divinity School at Yale and developing there a new program for Educational Leadership and Ministry. Even in those dark years between Fr. Bradford's departure and my arrival, when Tony acceded to Bishop Shaw's request that he be the Priest-in-Charge and guide All Saints' through the troubled waters, he would accept no compensation for the gargantuan task he had undertaken.

Tony was certainly a man of strong opinions and of strong emotions. He knew what he believed and shared it freely, often bluntly. And he loved passionately: God, Our Lady, his family, his students, and us, his companions on this earthly pilgrimage. As a preacher, he both elucidated and motivated. Certainly part of his power in the pulpit was his willingness to admit his own weaknesses and struggles. He too was in the trenches, fighting, experiencing the wounds of battle.

Some years ago I started my Christmas Eve sermon by talking about the last days of a parishioner who had died just several days before. Whit Whitridge was a dear man, a stalwart of our weekday Masses. I told of some of those visits and giving Last Rites to him as he was surrounded by family. I then remarked that preaching about death and the Last Rites was certainly an unusual start to a Christmas Eve sermon. Following the Mass, a young man who had gone to Roxbury Latin came up and said to me it didn't seem very unusual to him: it just sounded like I'd spent a lot of time around Fr. Jarvis. He went on to say that the Headmaster's address at the beginning of each school year boiled down to three points: welcome back, remember you're going to die;

have a good year. Tony knew that this life is a gift, that our time here is limited, and that what we do with it matters. And he held out that call to strive for the good, the true, the beautiful, the holy.

It was not incidental that Fr. Godderz would conclude his tribute to Tony with an anecdote from a Roxbury Latin old boy. If Kerry Brennan had good reason to conclude that Tony had tended his school as if it were his parish, the clergy and congregation of All Saints, Ashmont, experienced Tony as their headmaster. By all accounts Tony was as exacting of his clerical colleagues as he was of his faculty at Roxbury Latin. In all things, in both realms, Tony was attentive to detail, to decorum, and to what he felt was essential quality.

The All Saints choral program has for years been celebrated for its excellence, an excellence ardently supported by Tony. To the choristers, choir director, and organist, Tony's close attention was deeply appreciated, but at times daunting—a condition that would not surprise any of Tony's colleagues at school. Accompanying Fr. Godderz's tribute to Tony at his death was this remembrance by All Saints organist Andrew Sheranian:

When I first arrived at All Saints as the assistant organist in Lent of 1998, Fr. Jarvis was the Priest-in-Charge. As a freshman in college at the time, I sometimes slept a little later than I should have on Sunday mornings, and as a result, one Sunday I showed up for mass unshaven. After I played the closing organ voluntary, I tried to sneak past Fr. Jarvis, who at that moment was greeting parishioners in the Tower – but he suddenly broke away from the conversation he was having to grab me by the forearm and say, "Young man, do you think you could find the time to shave before coming to mass?" Perhaps this is one reason why I have since grown a beard?

Fr. Jarvis loved sacred music with every fiber of his being. It clearly played a principal role in his spiritual life. When the choir sang during mass, he didn't simply listen: he prayed. It was obvious to me that he felt a part of what the choir was doing. Last year, the choir sang a very simple motet by Mozart: his popular setting of "Ave verum corpus". After mass, Fr. Jarvis took me aside to tell me that he knew exactly what stops I had used on the organ as I was accompanying the motet during the Mass, just by listening. He knew that I had used the Clarinet stop on the Skinner organ, on an inner voice of the organ part, during the last two measures of the piece. This was no passive listening he was engaged in: he actively listened to every note, intently and prayerfully, letting it penetrate his soul.

Not only was Fr. Jarvis passionate about the Anglican choral tradition, he was also an ardent lover of congregational hymns, and I know that he had a great portion of the Hymnal committed to memory. I observed countless occasions when, as he processed into the chancel at the beginning of mass, he could confidently sing the hymn, without carrying a hymnal. He memorized the melody of the hymns, the texts, and, the tenor parts as well! He loved singing harmony on the inner verses of the hymns. He entered into worship with his whole body, mind, and soul: his devotion to our particular tradition was constantly evident.

I always craved Fr. Jarvis' approval, and would try to seek him out after mass to determine if he had approved of the music that particular Sunday. When choosing the choral music and the hymns, I frequently asked myself "How will Fr. Jarvis react if I schedule this anthem/motet/hymn?" His encouragement meant the world to me, and I strove to keep the standard of music-making high enough to satisfy him, a priest who had been shaped by his experiences at St. John's College in Cambridge (UK), which boasts one of the finest choirs in the world!

It became obvious to all of us who worked with him that Fr. Jarvis had a weakness for music from the Victorian period. In my time at Ashmont, I have uncovered and dusted-off a good number of Victorian hymns from the Hymnal. When-

ever I did so, Fr. Jarvis would find me after Mass, take hold of my arm and say "Ah, Queen Victoria would have felt right at home at today's mass! Bravo, and keep it coming!" Since I knew from this that he loved Victorian music, I planned a setting of the Te Deum by a little-known American composer from that period (Arthur Foote) to be sung on Trinity Sunday a few years back. Not only was Foote active during the Victorian era, he was a Bostonian, included in the group of composers called the "Boston Six", which included noted Victorian-era composers Horatio Parker and Amy Beach. Needless to say, I'd done my homework, and I assumed that Fr. Jarvis would be in raptures about that year's setting of the Te Deum. Boy, was I wrong! "That has got to be the ugliest setting of the Te Deum I have ever heard in my whole life, and I hope you never do it again!" At least one always knew where one stood with Fr. Jarvis!

He expected excellence because he knew that excellence in liturgy helps to create an atmosphere of transcendence, which helps to draw the worshipper closer to God. I never heard Fr. Jarvis make an error in the chanting of the Gospel, which he always did with such distinctive style. I got the impression that he took great pride in chanting the gospel, especially if that week's portion included a question or two. When a question occurs in the chanting of the Gospel, the tone dips down a semi-tone for the duration of the question, and then slides back up to the reciting tone at the end of the question. He took great delight in executing those questions, and he expected everyone else who was involved in carrying out the liturgy to bring the same level of exactitude and presence to their roles as he always brought to his. And, who can forget his chanting of the Exsultet at the Easter Vigil? "This is the night…"

I thank God that I was able to walk a few steps of this earthly pilgrimage with Fr. Tony Jarvis, who made an indelible impression on me and my work. May we never forget his example of commitment, passion, and prayerfulness.

KNOWING
TONY JARVIS

_____

You could not spend an hour with Tony without being struck by his distinctive qualities—the strength and clarity of his opinions, the sense he conveyed of being vividly with you but also of dwelling in another era—but those qualities in themselves do not convey the stimulation and the pleasure of being in his company. As I have probably made clear by now, I knew Tony well and for a long time. I know I have from time to time referred to him, without much reflection, as my "best" friend, and I would not be surprised if from time to time Tony referred to me that way. But the "best" designation is not important. Truer to say I have not had a better friend than Tony.

I believe the realization that a person within the constellation of one's relationships is a "friend" is more a discovery than a decision. Some people open themselves up to you and invite you to open up to them in a way that others don't. There is an element of mystery to friendship, or as some would put it, chemistry. I am willing to accept that some people set out to make—

forge—friendships intentionally, but in my personal experience friendship, often to my surprise, *happens*, a gift received if not necessarily sought or deserved.

As I relayed earlier in my account of getting to know Tony as we began our teaching lives together in Cleveland, he revealed from the outset a number of admirable traits—hard work on many fronts, well developed aesthetic preferences, considered, intelligent conversation—it was easy to admire, but he was much more than admirable. I have already noted that he was confoundingly generous materially, but more important to me and consequential for the work that I would go on to do, Tony was generous with his *attention.* I have never known anyone who listened more closely to what I said or read more closely what I wrote. There is no way to describe how stimulating that kind of attention is to further, better thought.

I remember being newly home from Cambridge and getting back to work at University School. I had just finished my doctoral requirements and was preparing to send out parts of my dissertation for publication in scholarly journals. One of them was the *Anglican Theological Review*, and because Tony was ardently Anglican, I asked him if he would look over what I was considering submitting. He not only read the drafts I gave him overnight, he had annotated them and suggested some minor stylistic improvements. If memory serves, he thought, no doubt correctly, that I over-used dashes. But mainly he conveyed to me a terrific interest in the points I was making, and he expressed it with an enthusiasm that gave me the impression that maybe *I* was interesting.

This quality of close attention never flagged in the fifty years of our friendship. I would go on to write many more manuscripts, including some novels, stories, poems, and non-fiction books about children and schools, and with no exception I can remember, Tony read all of them prior to publication. There were occasional concerns he wanted me to consider, and I did, but what he mostly conveyed was appreciation. If there was something I felt was concealed but at the heart of the poem or story I sent to Tony, he noted it at once. I have been blessed by other helpful early readers of my work, but none more consistently and more helpfully than Tony. I can recall perhaps a dozen times when I lived in Cleveland and he in Boston when I had just mailed him some draft of recent work. I was always more than eager to hear what he thought, and as if he sensed this, he would call me on the phone to report the second he had finished reading. He was otherwise not a frequent telephone caller, preferring to post letters and quick notes. It would have been unbearable for me to receive this continuing generosity without suppressing the certainty that these attentions were coming from the otherwise busiest, most heavily committed person I knew.

Then there was Tony's sheer physical energy. While never really a sportsman—there had been no Little League or Youth Soccer in his boyhood Painesville—and while never engaged in a considered exercise program, Tony was always fit and trim. After his move to Boston, I would see him mainly on weekends when my family and I were on vacation on the Cape. Our days spent together involved walking, literally, all over Cambridge and Boston. Tony seemed to know every used bookstore in both cities. He was also a tireless museum goer, and his endurance beholding exhibit after exhibit exceeded mine. I remember days where we must have hiked ten miles on both sides of the Charles River, our stops broken up by welcome restaurant meals, always Tony's treat because "you have a family and children to look after."

Years later, when we were both involved in the business of the International Boys' Schools Coalition, the annual conferences of which were hosted abroad on alternate years, Tony and I would spend similar, to me, exhausting days visiting the cultural and historic sites of London or Cape Town or Sydney or Auckland. More than a few of these sight-seeing marathons occurred at Tony's insistence after all-night flights to those cities during which I never seemed to be able to sleep, a problem Tony either did not share or did not mention. Though it was a decade ago, I can still summon up in my legs and feet what felt like the terminal exhaustion of trying to keep up with Tony as he made his way for six hours through every chamber of the Auckland War Memorial Museum, held rapt by the exhibits documenting New Zealand's and Great Britain's mutual sacrifices in the World Wars. Whatever historic site we visited, if there were brochures to be read, Tony read them; if there were headphones to document the background of what was on view, Tony listened. None of this seem effortful for him. I think he was a natural learner, the way some people are natural athletes.

Even when days spent together began with an early breakfast, conversation never flagged. There always seemed to be one more urgent thing to report. With Tony conversation could go freely anywhere. Tony seemed to me unshockable and on that account an especially good listener. However much his talks and sermons celebrated the narrow road, the harder life, and dedication to the needs of others, there was no prudish disinclination on his part to explore and to understand lives lived otherwise, including lives wasted and ruined.

Tony was a constant reader, from his middle years onward mostly history and biography, fiction only rarely. He subscribed to both American and British book reviews, and he often had read and sent me books I wanted to read before they were published in the United States. From the outset of our friendship he would hand and, later, mail me books he had just finished and thought I would like, and he was almost always right. He knew that I was interested in books about school life, famous or infamous teachers, and school foundings. Most of the school books I have now collected were gifts from Tony.

His recommendations could be surprising. When I was first getting to know him, I was fascinated that a convinced Christian was reading what I felt were the darkest fictions imaginable: Camus's *Stranger* and *The Plague*, Sartre's *Nausea* and *No Exit.* He insisted on teaching some of those books. Imaginatively at least, I think Tony needed to go to the darkest places, to contend with characters who could find nothing affirmative in life and who challenged the notion that there was any such thing. Like Flannery O'Connor, whom I don't think Tony read, Tony saw abjectly awful lives as negative evidence of divinity.

One day in 1982 he called to tell me he had just sent me a book I *had* to read. It was *Edie*, an extended oral history of the foreshortened life of Edie Sedgwick, compiled by George Plimpton, a distant cousin of his subject. Edie Sedgwick was the daughter of a wealthy but dissolute New England scion, Francis "Duke" Sedgwick. Sexually and otherwise abused as a child by her dysfunctional family, she studied art briefly in Boston before migrating to New York where she became a fixture in the emerging world of Andy Warhol and the countercultural characters who composed The Factory. She would be featured in a few of Warhol's chaotic underground films before being institutionalized for severe bulimia and a longstanding drug addiction. She died of an overdose of prescription sedatives in 1971 when she was 28. Presented from the perspectives of family members, friends, and other observers, Edie Sedgwick's life was, I agreed, arresting for its aimlessness and emptiness. On photographic evidence, she had a kitten-like beauty and, due to her eating disorders and drug intake, was model-slender. Taken together, the

accounts of her life reveal an unbroken series of sensa-
tions and distractions experienced in a mental fog, an
impression of utter lostness—an impression that went
deep with Tony.

A few years later, in 1986, Tony made another star-
tling recommendation. He had just gone out to see the
film *Sid and Nancy*, about the life and death of Sid Vi-
cious, the bassist for the punk band The Sex Pistols, and
of his girlfriend, Nancy. It took me a few minutes to
understand that Tony was serious. I have forgotten his
words, but the message was the same as it had been
with respect to *Edie*: the film had somehow conveyed
an elemental, if awful, *reality*. For me, in addition to being sub-musical, the then emerging punk phenomenon
represented a stagey adolescent nihilism I did not want
to support even to the extent of noticing it. I did not
go out to see the movie, but a year or two later when it
aired on a cable channel, I decided to watch it to see if
I could tell what had so moved Tony, and I think I did.
The film did nothing to romanticize the Sid and Nancy
characters, nor was there a suggestion that their delin-
quencies and personal misery were the result of insufficient nurture. Talentless and unapologetically trans-
gressive, both were addicted to heroin and other drugs.
Before falling in with Sid, Nancy had been a promis-

cuous grunge band groupie. Sid, both before and after his brief notoriety as a member of the calamitous Sex Pistols, was aimless, angry, and foul-mouthed, unable to get along with even his band mates. The film spared viewers nothing of the squalid dreariness of their lives. Both were dead at 21, Nancy having been stabbed by Sid, Sid of an overdose. For me, there *was* something gripping in this grim spectacle I had not wanted to watch: I could not stop wondering how a childhood—a life—could come to *that*.

Tony wanted to know. He was an effective counselor, I think, because of his willingness to take in what people, whether his boys at Roxbury Latin or his adult colleagues and parishioners, had to tell him without judgment. Despite so much outward—and genuine— rectitude, Tony always made me feel that I could share with him anything about my life, and at a few very low ebbs I did. Personally and professionally, Tony was the most reliable counsel I knew. Whatever problem I might disclose to him, his primary concern was always how I was managing, whether I was all right. Supported that way, one becomes a problem solver.

The longer I knew Tony, the more mutual acquaintances we formed. As I got to know them over the years, I came to understand that what I had imagined was my own privileged relationship with Tony was in fact widely shared. I would not be surprised at all if a dozen, if not dozens, of Tony's friends and colleagues feel they have a book's worth of remembrances of their distinctive friend. For again, knowing Tony Jarvis was not quite like knowing anybody else.

WIN

I met Win Bassett in the course of my guest teaching visits to Tony at Yale Divinity School. By the time I encountered him in Tony's classroom, he had established himself as a serious and accomplished scholar. As he would explain to me when I got to know him, Tony was the reason he had sought out the Yale program in educational leadership and ministry. Win struck me as an especially warm and decorous young man. In his mid-twenties he was, to my Yankee sensibilities, something of a Southern Gentleman, a stereotype he seemed eager to transcend. Born and raised in Martinsville, Virginia, he was valedictorian of his high school class. Awarded a full merit scholarship to North Carolina State University, he received B.S degrees in both general and electrical engineering. Setting aside further thoughts of engineering, he went on to study law at the University of North Carolina, where he became an editor of its *Law Review.* He would practice law for two years, first as a patent lawyer for a large firm, then as an assistant district attorney prosecuting criminal cases before deciding the law may not be his vocation. While he pondered what his next steps might be, he came into possession of Tony's *With Love and Prayers*—he does not recall how—which strengthened his resolve to explore a different career path. He learned that Tony now directed Yale's ELM program, and since Win was favorably disposed to teaching and a life in schools, he applied and was admitted.

Win first saw Tony in the flesh as he watched him participate on a panel addressing newly admitted students but who had not yet enrolled. The drive north to New Haven was his first experience of New England. Seeking reassurance that he was doing the right thing, he tracked down Tony in his office and asked if they could talk. As it happened, Tony was on his way out the door to another meeting, but something about Win's intensity persuaded him to change his mind. In an extended exchange that followed, Win confessed that he wasn't sure he knew what he was doing. The program seemed promising but, he admitted to Tony, he was "scared to death." According to Win, Tony did not even pause before answering, "Everything I have done in my life that mattered scared me to death."

"That conversation did it," Win told me. He enrolled in the program and, though he would not say it, proceeded to distinguish himself as one of the brightest lights in his class. He had for some time been writing and publishing poems as well as poetry reviews and criticism, some of which he shared with me. The intensity and craft of the poems reminded me of Gerard Manley Hopkins.

While he was at Yale, Win encountered Tony every day, beginning with the Morning Prayer service for the ELM students. In addition to seeing Tony in class, Win recalls nearly daily office visits and emails. "He took me seriously from day one." Part of the ELM program involved students identifying the kind of school vocations they wanted to pursue—chaplaincies, classroom teaching, administration. In one such conference with Tony, Win said he thought teaching high school classes might be the best fit for him. Tony surprised him by countering, "Why not be a headmaster?" Until that moment, Win told me, he had no prior thought of becoming a headmaster, but not long afterward the notion took root and is now his professional goal.

While he taught him at Yale and afterward, Tony paid close, and sometimes critical, attention to Win's progress. Tony would occasionally invite promising divinity students up to Boston to preach a guest sermon at All Saints, an honor and usually a memorable experience for those chosen. Win may have been the only student to have been invited twice. After Win's graduation from the Divinity School and having begun teaching duties at the Montgomery Bell Academy in Nashville, Win was invited by Tony to co-present with him a workshop on mentorship for that year's conference of the International Boys' Schools Coalition in Baltimore. I attended the workshop, and I thought both Tony and Win acquitted themselves impressively, though Win confided to me that Tony was very demanding as they attempted to collaborate and that "he almost gave up on me."

On May 5, 2019, Roxbury Latin Headmaster Kerry Brennan put together an appropriately elaborate memorial service for Tony, drawing together the extended school community, including present and past parents, colleagues, graduates, as well as various scholastic and clerical eminences from greater Boston. The invited guests exceeded the capacity of Rousmaniere Hall, so that later arrivals watched the proceedings on video from other locations on the campus. In addition to selected choral works, and excerpts from Tony's talks read by alumni, six figures from Tony's past were selected to address different dimensions of Tony's life. I talked about

Tony's early teaching in Cleveland. Tony's nephew Ned Smith, himself a headmaster of Episcopal High School in Houston, talked about Tony's place in his family. Harry Lewis, a former Roxbury Latin Board Chair and Dean of the College at Harvard, spoke about Tony's school leadership. Carolyn Peter, formerly head of Boston's Winsor School, remembered Tony's professional support and friendship. Mike Pojman, Tony's assistant headmaster, talked about Tony as a colleague. Win Bassett was invited to talk about Tony's post retirement work at Yale.

Win was honored but also a little startled to be asked to contribute. His remarks began:

When I discovered Father Jarvis's With Love and Prayers*, which contributed to my leaving the field of law to train under this giant to become a schoolmaster like him, I never could have imagined that I would be asked one day to say few kind words about my teacher, mentor, and friend.*

I will call him Father Jarvis this afternoon because I always did. Two years ago, someone in the school world told me that if I wanted to be taken seriously as "Tony's" peer, I should refer to him as "Tony." I never was nor ever will be his peer, and when I told Father Jarvis what this person advised, he said, in his most loving way, something I cannot repeat to you this afternoon.

Win went on to recount how, after he left Yale, Tony kept in touch and sent him "with glorious frequency" books he thought Win would enjoy. Until he died, Tony would continue to play an outsized part in Win's life. When Win married his Divinity School classmate Gracie in Nashville, Tony was one of the priests invited to preside over the service, offering the marital blessing and joining their hands. Tony specified in his will that Win should have his pick of volumes from his personal library, including the cost of shipping his selections to Nashville.

One of the books Tony wanted Win to have was Stephen Spender's *World Within World* which opened to a page on which Tony had folded down the corner. The page recounted Spender's impression of his boarding school music teacher when Spender was nine. Win concluded his remembrance at the memorial by sharing the passage:

He had a manner more brusque than that of other masters, but less frightening. It had more of the warm great world than of the refrigerated school. While he conducted our singing, I used to stare at his domed bald head with the clusters of hair on each side and at the back, and pray that when I grew up I would be bald. For the child unquestionably attributes beauty to whom he loves.

Win concluded: "I pray when I grow up that I will be half the Christ-servant, schoolmaster, mentor, man of letters and human that Father Jarvis was. For this boy unquestioningly attributes beauty to whom he loves."

As I write this, Win is completing his sixth year at the Montgomery Bell Academy, where he is teaching English, coaching runners, and serving as an associate dean of the high school. Up until his death Tony continued to correspond weekly with Win. Tony told me a number of times, including in the course of our final meal together, that he hoped I would keep up with Win, because he believed he was certain to be a great headmaster.

CAROLYN

Carolyn Peter had recently retired from the Directorship of Winsor School when she offered her remembrance of Tony at his memorial service. Because Winsor School girls and Roxbury Latin boys joined forces for drama and musical productions over the years, there was enough mutual business to require an agreeable working relationship between the respective school heads. In Tony's and Carolyn's case, the relationship evolved into a deep thirty-year friendship.

Carolyn began her remarks with an account of meeting Tony when he came to observe her as a prospective candidate for the Directorship of the Winsor School. Tony was at that time a Winsor trustee and member of the search committee for the new head:

I first met Tony in 1987, when he came to Lincoln School, where I was a teacher and head of upper school, to interview me for the position of Director of the Winsor School. We were certainly not friends yet, and he was a tough interviewer. As he told me some years later, I was NOT his first choice for Winsor, but he somehow changed his mind about me, and in July 1988, I came to Winsor…with much to learn about leading a school. Luckily, I think Tony felt some responsibility for me…

In the years to follow, as I came to know Tony well and our friendship grew, I understood why he was so loved and admired at Roxbury Latin School and beyond. There was a lot to love and admire about Tony, and I am only one among many to whom he expressed his generosity and compassion. Years ago when I was a trustee at RL, Tony spoke of headmastering at the end of a long and arduous board meeting. I tried to scribble down every word he said, and thereafter, each September at the opening of school, I returned to notes from that meeting for inspiration and courage. Tony spoke about the pressure created for any school head by the sheer number of school constituencies: trustees, faculty, parents, alumni, and students. He said not everyone understands why the head doesn't do everything he or she wants, yet each asserts a right to the headmaster's time and expects him to listen to the anger or worry or hurt. He spoke of bouts of exhaustion and inevitable isolation. He said that heads of school survive because they are idealists, seeing people and situations in terms of possibilities rather than simply as problems. He believed that being head of school is the world's best job, and he guided others to that understanding of their work.

As their friendship progressed, Carolyn could not help being charmed by his signature characteristics, including the forcefulness of his opinions and his inflexibility about reconsidering them. She came quickly to note his unapologetic tendency to hyperbole:

Years ago I began making a list of Tony's unequivocal statements, each of which I heard many times. Here are a few:

Upon completing the Robert Smith Theatre: "This is absolutely the last building I will ever put up."

At the end of October—every October: "I'm just hanging on by my fingernails."

Twice a year: "I've just had the worse parent conference of my life. I mean absolutely the worst."

At least twice a year, directed at me: "Only a wimp would close school for that little dusting of snow."

Usually in May: "I have just hired a teacher who walks on water."

Just before graduation each year: "This is the strongest class in the school's history."

And just when I needed it most, Tony would say, "Don't forget how much I love you."

Tony's and Carolyn's friendship continued unabated after their retirement from Roxbury Latin and Winsor. Their appreciation of one another is evident in this 2017 email exchange Carolyn shared with me:

Carolyn to Tony: *Dearest Tony, it was a great pleasure to see you yesterday. Thank you for inviting me to lunch at the elegant St. Botolph's Club and for sharing two such happy hours with me. I remember so many times that we had supper together when we were at RL and Winsor, and always I came away uplifted by your friendship and thoughtful conversation. That's just how I felt yesterday. I so much hope you continue to maintain good health. Regular [chemotherapy] infusions are no fun, but your presence in the world means so much to me—and to everyone who wants you to officiate at weddings, speak at conferences, write eulogies, and to be your friend. I count myself lucky that you are my continuing, enduring friend.*

Tony to Carolyn: *Dear, dear Carolyn, I too was happily recalling the dinners we had to share our tears (of sorrow and joy) when we were running the two best schools on earth. I always felt there was no effort to cover things over. We could truly and honestly share our burdens. What wonderful times those were even in some dark hours. But these are now good times and it was a great joy for me to share my present burdens. I have always felt blessed by your friendship.*

A few months before he died, Tony emailed Carolyn to ask if they might get together for lunch. He wanted to tell her personally that since his chemotherapy was no longer effective, he was going to let his symptoms run their course, and that he had only a few more months to live. Unaware of this and recovering from an accident herself, Carolyn wrote back to ask if they could postpone the lunch date for a few weeks, Tony's response was the last message she would receive from him:

Dearest Carolyn, the reason I wanted to break bread with you was to share with you, as I promised to do when the time came, that I have ended chemo (doing me no good and making me very sick) and that I have 9 to 18 months to live. I am very happy about this. I hated the idea of old age and the inability to be doing things for people day by day. God has arranged things beautifully, and I shall not face a useless old age lingering about. I am very happy about these things—how could I not be after the happiest possible life… Much love, as ever, Tony

TYLER

I don't think there are many people who knew him who would challenge the assertion that to know Tony was to have a formative presence in your life. For more than a few, Tony became the most formative presence. I have referred earlier to Tony's guidance of his ELM student Tyler Montgomery as he progressed to his ordination, but that story is longer and deeper.

Like probably most college seniors considering career options, Tyler was not at all clear about what he wanted his life's work to be. He was also struggling with his personal faith life, to the extent that his father, a private school headmaster and a friend of Tony's and mine, suggested that he get in touch with Tony for counsel. Tyler duly sent Tony a letter describing his concerns, and Tony responded with an invitation to visit him in New Haven. Just before heading off to Costa Rica to serve in the Peace Corps, Tyler drove to Connecticut and spent a full day touring the Divinity School, attending Tony's class, and in the evening sharing a three-hour restaurant dinner, during which Tyler told me he recounted his "entire tumultuous journey through Penn." When he had finished, Tony told him with an arresting certainty that he, Tyler, "had all the essential qualities of a priest." The idea of becoming a priest, Tyler said, had never occurred to him before. But once proposed, the idea struck a chord. Upon completion of his Peace Corps assignment two years later, he enrolled in the Divinity School's ordination program and began his studies with Tony.

The intimate size of the ELM program enabled Tony to know each of his students well, and that was certainly the case with Tyler. Tyler remembers that Tony was at once impressed by and also concerned about his "earnestness" and took pains to test the depth of his various convictions by challenging them vigorously from the opposite perspective. In time Tyler came to see that this "sparring" was an intentional strategy on Tony's part to clarify and firm up what he, Tyler, believed. In a way familiar to me, Tyler described how this intellectual sparring would also devolve into good natured teasing and joking, noting that nothing seemed to please Tony more than parrying students' gibes at his expense. For Tyler, Tony's company in class or in individual conferences was, among other things, a lot of fun. On occasion Tyler recalls being a little wondrous at how easily and gladly Tony could slip out of his clerical persona. The Divinity School refectory tended to be cramped during the lunch hour, and in the course of one of them Tony and Tyler were sharing a table elbow-to-elbow with other students and faculty. As their banter progressed in the direction of hilarity, Tyler responded with what he thought was an appropriate counter-insult to what Tony has just said, which delighted Tony and made him laugh—and (as Tyler remembers) to practically shout out, "Montgomery, you are such an *asshole.*"

Tyler's relationship to Tony went deeper than teaching and advising, sparring and joking. There was a time midway through Tyler's progress through the Divinity School program when his world seemed to collapse. He had fallen in love with a woman he thought he would marry, but she suddenly and unexpectedly broke off the relationship. Explaining to Tony what happened, Tyler broke down in tears. As did Tony, which Tyler said made him feel "validated" in his heartbreak.

Tony's guidance and friendship with Tyler would

continue undiminished until Tony died. Tony encouraged and also tested Tyler's decisions to take on his first professional positions, as chaplain at the College of William and Mary, then at Woodbury Forest School, a boys' boarding school in Virginia.

In the final months of his life when he was disposing of his possessions, Tony called Tyler to ask if he would like to have his Ackermann print of King's College, Cambridge, noting that it had become valuable over the years, and he wanted someone to have it who wouldn't go off and sell it. Today the picture hangs in Tyler's living room—but it is not the most valued gift Tony gave him. In October of 2018, when Tyler drove north to attend Tony's funeral Mass at All Saints, Ashmont, Rector Godderz surprised him by telling him he had something to give him and handed him a package containing a photograph of Tony as a young priest. Affixed to the back of the picture was a personal note from Tony written on Roxbury Latin stationery and dated a few days before his death. The note thanked Tyler for a tribute he had recently offered in Tony's remembrance. Tyler's tribute had concluded:

There were two pictures on my grandfather's desk for as long as I knew him. The first was of his late father, whom he adored. The second was of Prof. Milliken, who took him in as a son and introduced him to schools and his vocation.

Your picture is on my desk.
With love and prayers,

Tyler

SALLY

A few days after I returned home from Tony's memorial service, I received a warm note from a woman I did not know, Sally Muspratt, thanking me for my remarks. She identified herself as an old friend of Tony's and noted appreciatively the pleasure it must have been for Tony and me to put together our Western Civilization course as we were finding our feet as teachers. Some combination of her name and her warm regard for Tony roused memory, and I recalled Tony telling me some time ago and with some excitement about a girl he had liked in his college days resurfacing in his world as a Roxbury Latin mother. I remember no details beyond his gladness it had occurred. I wrote back thanking her for her generous remarks about my talk and mentioned that Tony had spoken of her fondly.

When I was gathering my thoughts for this reflection about Tony's life, it occurred to me that in our long acquaintance Tony had shared few anecdotes and almost no memories of friends and loves from his school and university days. He had been lonely at St. Mark's. He had worked hard at his studies there and subsequently. The physical and architectural impact of St. Mark's as well as Harvard and Cambridge universities had gone deep with him, but for a man of so many close friendships, almost none of them seem to have been forged in his school days. Hoping she might shed some light, I wrote back to Sally telling her I was considering this project and wondered if she cared to share her impressions of Tony as a very young man.

She was indeed willing, and while her memories of their shared experiences at both Harvard and Cambridge corroborated my picture of him then as relatively unto himself, the connection he made with Sally, including its more than half century duration, reveals something of his signature commitment to anyone once befriended. Sally began her reminiscence:

Although neither he nor I was ever at the center of the other's life, we shared so many interests that I think we were both aware of the possibility that we might come to mean more to each other. This never happened, but my admiration and affection for him never changed.

He and I discovered at Harvard that we had a lot in common. I too grew up in Ohio and was sent to boarding school to have my Horizons Broadened, as my parents' had been. My two older sisters had gone off to Farmington [Miss Porter's School] willingly, but I knew I would be extremely homesick. Eventually I came to love the academic work, and I made some good friends. Three of us came on to Radcliffe together.

Sunday Night Evening Prayers at school meant enough to us that our first Sunday at Radcliffe, we went together to an Evensong at Christ Church, Cambridge. I first met Tony at a coffee hour atfter church one morning later in the year.

Besides both coming from Ohio and having similar feelings about being outshone by our more sophisticated Eastern boarding school friends, we had in common our major in English History and Lit., a small department that thought very well of itself and set us apart from (and we felt far above!) those who coasted through the less demanding straight English or History programs.

Sally reported one dramatic incident from their Harvard days:

My clearest memory of Tony at Harvard comes from our senior year. My parents had given me a little red Ford, and Tony and another Radcliffe girl and I decided to drive back to

Ohio for Christmas. Tony was driving when we hit an invisible patch of black ice; the car tipped over in a ditch. None of us was badly hurt, but I lost my two front teeth and the other girl cracked a rib. I think Tony's parent picked us up and invited me to spend the night. That was my only meeting with them. I remember they were very kind and sensibly didn't blame Tony for the accident. It is possible that his dislike of driving began with this accident.

Whether or not dating from the accident, Tony did dislike driving and though he would maintain a small, inexpensive car throughout his adult life, he rarely used it, preferring public transportation when necessary and walking when possible.

From Harvard Tony and Sally would both go on to Cambridge University, Sally to Newnham College, one the University's two women's colleges, Tony to St. John's. Deeply engaged in their respective studies, they got together only occasionally, usually to attend choral concerts. Once, Sally recalls, they decided to attend a performance of Handel's *Messiah* in London during a winter break. Arriving a little late and rushing upstairs to their inexpensive seats high up in the concert hall, Sally remembers fainting from the exertion, "but just briefly. Neither one of wanted to miss a note."

For the most part Tony and Sally went their separate ways at Cambridge. Sally confesses to sharing none of Tony's Anglophilia and was imply bemused by his interest in Charles the First. While they were both dazzled by finding themselves genuine members of the university instead of mere tourists, Sally found living there sharpened her appreciation of being an American, while Tony's Cambridge deepened his admiration for all things English.

She also remembers being impressed that Tony outperformed her on the history Tripos exams on which Cambridge degrees are based. If Tony and Sally saw less of each other at Cambridge, it was possibly in part because Sally had met the man she would eventually marry.

After returning to the United States, Sally and Tony saw little of each other until the late 1980s. She and her husband had agreed to part, and they turned together to Tony for help choosing schools for their sons.

We both counted on Tony for good advice and were relieved when Matt was accepted at RL. I found a house near the school so he and later his brother could walk to school and I could pursue my new career in landscape design without worrying about carpools. We were both very grateful for the care Tony took of our sons. When we met at plays and sporting events, he always greeted us with fresh, perceptive comments on how they were getting on. Like so many parents of RL boys, we had real evidence that Tony did know and love each of his students. Nothing could have mattered more to either of us.

While we had chosen the school for our boys because of the excellent role models provided by the men who taught there—no women teachers then—I was surprised to learn that mothers were only barely tolerated on campus. I was anxious not to presume on my previous friendship with Tony. Aside from helping with the annual yard sale and attending school functions, I saw very little of him.

They did not lose touch. Sally and her boys attended both the 25th and 50th anniversaries of Tony's ordination to the priesthood. She loved the services at All Saints, Dorchester, but couldn't help smiling when she found a small ikon of Charles the First illuminated in an unobtrusive niche.

In the last decade of Tony's life, their connection was renewed and deepened.

We didn't really get to talk until our fiftieth Harvard reunion—I was amazed how much he remembered about my family. He knew about his cancer by our 55th reunion. He talked about it freely…It was also a pleasure to hear about his happiness at Yale in the years after he left RL.

In his last years he invited me to lunch several times. I loved hearing more about his life. I was astounded to learn of his great friendship with Virginia Wing, the Headmistress of Winsor School. I knew vaguely about their collaboration on joint theatrical performances for their two schools—but friendship! In her first year as headmistress Miss Wing hired me for my first teaching job when I came down from Cambridge. I never lost my dread of falling short of the expectations of that then stern lady.

Another happy recent memory is being invited to a gathering at his beautiful rooms in Dorchester and given a tour of his library and extraordinary collection of English prints and memorabilia. These meetings seemed part of a plan to say goodbye gently to everyone he had ever known.

I was deeply impressed by the fulness of the life he had chosen and by his bravery in getting through the horrible treatments he suffered. I do not think either of us spent any time thinking of roads not taken…he understood that his freedom from domestic ties enabled him to focus without distraction on his church and on his school and so to do the enormous amount of meticulous work that meant so much to him and was so helpful to others.

What a life!

Mike

I met and came to like Mike Pojman in the mid-1970s when he joined the faculty of University School to teach math. At the time, well trained math and science teachers were in short supply, and we were especially pleased to find Mike, a Greater Cleveland boy who had recently completed his studies at John Carroll University, a Jesuit college. Just after he was hired, I remember our headmaster calling me into his office to tell me that "this *Pojman*," whose college transcript he had been reviewing, "has got a higher verbal S.A.T. than most of my English faculty."

Mike impressed me right away for being conscientious about his class preparations and for the depth of his investment in individual students, especially those who were struggling to get by. Because he was so young, some of his more confident students tested him, but by taking them seriously and teaching them rigorously he won their respect. I remember thinking: *keeper.*

But as it happened, he got away. A valued presence at University School after just a few years and sure of his teaching vocation, Mike determined he wanted to test himself in a setting beyond Cleveland where he had spent his entire life. Aware that many of the country's leading private schools were in New England, he applied to teach at a number of top tier boarding schools, because he liked the idea of round the clock immersion in school life. And though it was a day school, he also applied to Roxbury Latin, because he had heard about our departed colleague Tony Jarvis and was intrigued.

Mike had pretty much decided to teach and coach sailing at St. George's School in Rhode Island when he interviewed at Roxbury Latin. Having gotten lost driving trying to find the school from Cambridge, he was almost late and more than a little flustered when Tony greeted him for the first time. Expecting to be grilled, Mike was surprised that Tony offered only expansive, friendly conversation as they made their way back into Cambridge for an extended lunch. Mike recalls being asked only one job-related question: "What do you see yourself doing in five years?" Mike had no idea, but however he hedged, Tony offered him a job before they had finished eating.

What Mike would be doing five years hence was making a place for himself at the center of Roxbury Latin School life. He was given a big job from the outset: four courses, including three separate preparations in math, chemistry, and physical science. In addition, he was assigned to advise both the student newspaper, *the Tripod*, and the school yearbook, the quality of which had been flagging. Along with his other colleagues, Mike would look after his cohort of personal advisees, a job he attended to with special dedication. The small enrollment of Roxbury Latin requires most boys to be multiply and heavily extended in the school's extra-curricular life. If Mike was going to work productively with the young journalists in his charge, he would have to carve out time to work with them in the evening and on the weekends. In so doing, he established the kind of immersion in school life he had hoped to find in a boarding school. The depth of his commitments to the boys inside and outside of the classroom did not go unnoticed. In a faculty highly regarded by the boys generally, Mike Pojman soon found an honored place.

While Tony was headmaster I don't think a year passed without his telling me something to the effect that Mike was his luckiest hire, that he was doing heroic service, that he was a "saint." After a few years Mike was elevated to Director of Studies, though with little reduction to his teaching and extra-curricular load, and a few years after that, Tony named him his Assistant Headmaster.

Mike's regard for Tony was mutual. When I asked Mike recently to summarize his relationship to Tony as it evolved over the quarter century they worked together, he wrote me the following:

Tony was a tough taskmaster, but he was an inspiring headmaster. Being around him was never relaxing, but it was always stimulating. I owe my career to Tony. He gave me many opportunities to grow as a school man, and he steered me in the right direction over and over again. I had no idea what he meant when during my second or third year at the school he said to me, "You are the best thing that happened to me as headmaster," but I ultimately came to see that it meant we shared the same values and had the same vision for the school. He saw me as an ally. Wisely, however, I never saw myself as an equal, nor did I ever presume to overstep my position as Assistant Headmaster during the last half of Tony's tenure…

Mike was the last eulogist to address the audience at Tony's memorial service. His tribute testified not only to his admiration of Tony's work but for the enlivening *tone* in which he carried it out. As indicated already, Tony managed to combine a resolute firmness with a saving lightness. You were sometimes closest to Tony when you were kidding him. Mike's appreciation of that quality was evident in his reminiscence of Tony on the job.

Let's start with [Tony's] vision for this school—razor sharp, laser focused. Tony understood that unless we had a consensus view of who we are, we would never become what we wanted to be, what we claimed to be. He made it his mission to articulate that vision and to build that consensus. And he relished the task. He had an iron will, of course, and an unshakable sense of right and wrong—which often meant that he was right and you were wrong.

Had he been in attendance, no one would have laughed harder than Tony as Mike shared a succession of anecdotes of their work together. It is Roxbury Latin's practice to have graduating seniors vote to determine who would be designated valedictorian; elsewhere the honor tends to be conferred on the senior with the highest scholastic average. One of Mike's duties had been to preside over the meeting in which the seniors made their selection. One year Mike recalled that Tony was appalled by the boy selected and confronted Mike about it.

"How could you let that happen?" he demanded. "Democracy?" I replied.

On the other hand, although he must have been apprehensive, he did not preview the boy's valedictory address before he delivered it at the Closing Exercises. And by the way, while it was well understood that Tony believed in freedom of schoolboy speech in the narrowest of terms, he never once asked to see an article for The Tripod before its publication.

In the daily life of the school, Tony's word was law, his reality became reality, just his saying so made it so. I once had the temerity to challenge the provenance of something he regularly attributed to our Puritan founder, John Eliot. Undaunted, Tony responded, "Well, if he didn't say it, he would have."

Mike went on to celebrate Tony's distinctive touch with parents.

Tony orchestrated [parent] meetings with precision, and going in he always knew what he wanted coming out. There was a particularly challenging back-and-forth with a couple of unreasonable parents, who recklessly wheeled out one lame excuse after another to justify their son's bad behavior. The boy really was a terror. Tony never lost his cool as tensions rose, and of course he carried the day. After some uncomfortable back-and-forth, the tide turned decisively when he looked at them directly and proclaimed, "We love your son…but we don't like him." That was classic Jarvis shock and awe. But it was OK, because it turned out they didn't like him either. So, after a period of parental reconstruction, Tony concluded the meeting with a characteristically pastoral sendoff: "Now go in peace," he said as they got up to leave. "And tell your son you love him. Today. He needs to hear you say the words."

It would have been a mistake, and Mike did not make it, to conclude his remembrance of Tony without a reckoning about his relationship to the boys of the school.

Tony loved these boys, and he understood them—what they needed, what they wanted, what brought them joy, and what caused them pain. He forged a natural bond with them, I think, because in the grown-up Tony there were the remains of an impulsive adolescent—and a petulant juvenile at that. He struggled to tame that unruly child his whole life. Tony could reach into the minds and hearts of R.L. boys because he could relate to them—connect with their best or even their worse selves. He enjoyed them, untangled them, consoled them—but never indulged them.

Two years ago, [Headmaster Kerry Brennan] graciously invited Tony to speak to the school about "whatever was in his heart"—just as Tony had instructed so many Hall speakers over the years. Of course, he commanded the room. He was in top form, and delivered a profoundly moving address. But I was certain I heard his voice quiver as he was finishing his remarks. It was the only time I had seen him lose his composure at the lectern.

"Were you feeling nostalgic?" I asked him afterwards.

"No," he said. "I was just looking out and seeing all those beautiful faces."

In a recent letter to me Mike wrote that, close as their working relationship had been at the school, their friendship actually grew and deepened after Tony's retirement. They would meet often for lunches and dinners. Mike was the last friend to visit Tony before he died. Now Roxbury Latin's Associate Headmaster, he is completing his 41st year of service to the school.

KERRY

In the spring of 1978 Tony was on the lookout for a new music director, not an easy post to fill because someone with the necessary musical skill set may not have the range to teach in other disciplines or to coach athletic teams, both of which are required of most Roxbury Latin faculty. The position was still open and there were no promising prospects when, in the course of a casual phone conversation between Kay Hubbard, Tony's administrative assistant, and Ed Wall, the Amherst College Admissions Director, Kay happened to ask Wall if he knew of any musically talented Amherst grads who might be interested in directing choirs at Roxbury Latin. Remarkably, Wall knew just such a person.

Kerry Brennan had at that point just graduated from Amherst and having made an impressive undergraduate mark there as a singer and choral director, was given a one-year appointment to be a faculty Associate in Music and Acting Director of the Amherst College Glee club as well as a new co-ed choir he had formed in recognition of the college's going co-ed in 1976. Kerry was elated to get the post and to be spending a year preparing his chorus for a series of ambitious performances. He was in final-week rehearsals for a challenging joint concert with Mount Holyoke's choir when he got a telephone call from Kay Hubbard asking with some urgency if he could come to Roxbury Latin to talk about a position teaching music. Surprised and also a little intrigued, Kerry explained that he was heavily extended that week and also that he had been offered a musical position at another school but had not yet responded. Struck by Kay's insistence that he come anyway—no one at the school at this point had even seen his resume—Kerry cleared his schedule and drove to West Roxbury.

Reflecting back on that time, Kerry recalls a vague vocational sense that, since his undergraduate experience had been so satisfying, he would probably go on to graduate school in music, then look for a choral music post in a college as much like Amherst as he could find. At the same time, the prospect of working with younger students was appealing. Growing up in a lively working-class family in Schenectady, New York, he had, while still in high school, directed a youth choir in his Catholic church, while serving also as organist and choir director at a nearby Protestant church. In what was not very much spare time, he managed to teach piano lessons for pocket money.

Against the possibility of being a high school music teacher, he took an exam that would temporarily certify him to teach in New York public schools. At Amherst he had befriended a number of students who had attended private schools, and he decided to check out opportunities there. The college alumni office had a Porter Sargent private school directory, so he made some inquiries, followed through with applications, and, given the promise indicated by his scholastic record at Amherst and by his already established musical acumen, he was offered a job teaching music at The Peddie School in Hightstown, New Jersey. The Peddie headmaster at the time was an Amherst graduate, which Kerry took as a good omen.

Good omen notwithstanding, Kerry made his way to The Roxbury Latin School, resume in hand, to meet the headmaster who seemed so anxious to talk to him before he committed himself elsewhere. He would meet with five members of the school's senior staff that day, but it was his interview with Tony that became indelible. In a recent letter to me Kerry wrote that his first impression of Tony was that he was "young, energetic, preppy-looking."

In retrospect I realize I was being offered an authentic view of Tony—vibrant, opinionated, dismissive, charming, clear. Early in our conversation, after hearing about my conducting experience, church music positions, organ, piano, and voice training, he was convinced that I would be fine for the director of music position. "Well clearly you could do the music job, but that isn't the whole position. What else could you possibly teach?" I was surprised. Kay Hubbard had not indicated something else was needed. "I see that you are a political science major. I don't believe in political science." After asking me about what kind of algebra student I was (I learned later that Tony thought anybody should be able to teach algebra!) he said, "What kind of writer are you?" I allowed as I was a passable writer. "How about English? How about 8th grade English?" I knew enough to sound enthusi-

*astic about something that seemed a little terrifying. I said,
"That would be great."*

Kerry could not help but be knocked off balance by
Tony's directness—*I don't believe in political science!*—
and by what he assumed Kerry ought to be able to han-
dle as a Roxbury Latin colleague. What would turn out
to be enormously consequential for the next half century of Roxbury Latin is that each took an appreciative
measure of the other. Reflecting later, Kerry wrote that
Tony helped him to feel "that I was capable of tackling
almost anything in school life."

The following autumn Kerry would begin tackling
it: the glee club and smaller ensembles, three different
music classes, his English sections, and the Fourth (sev-
enth and eighth grades) basketball team.

*At 22, I wasn't that far away from the seniors Tony had
come to know and love and inspire, and he, I suspect like
me, realized that given the modesty of my blue-collar background that RL might be just the right fit. As I had come to
know independent schools—many quite fancy and composed
of boys and girls from moneyed families—I realized that I had
arrived at one in which I and my kind would feel comfortable.*

I was a public-school kid and, while I always had friendly relationships with my school principals, I got the sense that Tony and his job were dramatically different. Tony usually had good instincts about people, and I am so grateful for his charging into the possibility of my teaching English. English and music have accompanied me throughout my teaching career, and I could not have known how satisfying that would be. Nor could I have known that that fortuitous April meeting would result in my life's work. Nor could I ever have imagined that some day I would occupy the same role as Tony Jarvis—whose stature and influence in my life would grow every year I knew him.

Among other things, Tony's stature and influence inspired Kerry to think about being a school leader himself. He was given a year's leave to pursue a Klingenstein Fellowship at Columbia where he completed a study of the implications for well-developed arts programs in schools. As Tony predicted, or at least assumed, Kerry became an effective English teacher, and the school's choral program exceeded anything in school memory and was soon touring the country. After eight years at Roxbury Latin and thirty years old, Kerry, with Tony's blessing, offered his candidacy for the directorship of the Lower School (grades K-8) campus of University School, of which I would soon be headmaster. As it happened, I had already met Kerry, who had become a close friend of one of my former students who had gone on to Amherst. There were a number of appealing applicants for the Lower School job, all of them, with the exception of Kerry, well beyond 30 years old.

Tony and I discussed at length whether Kerry would be a good fit for our Lower School. He had more than charmed everyone he met in his initial interview. He impressively overcame some colleagues' concern about his youth, but there were lingering questions about his lack of experience in the elementary grades. I asked Tony what he thought. "Believe me," Tony had said, "He will rise to it," a prediction that proved true.

"But," Tony said, "There's something you need to know about Kerry."

"And that would be…"

"He has a very strong will."

"And…"

"That's all I can say. He knows what he wants, and he is not happy if he doesn't get it."

I could not resist: "So Tony, are you telling me I should be on my guard against a new colleague who knows what he wants and might be especially motivated to make it happen? Noted. Hard to imagine a person like that thriving in a school."

Tony cursed me roundly and said, "I stand by my recommendation, Hawley-bird."

For as long as he lived, Tony did stand by Kerry Brennan. In fact his greatest service to Kerry and to the school may be the least remarked. In 2004, after much deserved celebration and tribute, Tony departed from his post and from the larger world of the school in a way that made room for Kerry to take effective charge. It of course helped that the two men were devoted friends, and if there was nothing he could do to dim the fond memory of his service and his company, Tony took effective measures not to cast a shadow over what would prove to be a vigorous new chapter in the school's history.

Though Tony would take up residence not far away in his Dorchester rooms, he took pains not to be a presence on the campus. He turned his attention quickly to other business, first a few months of world travel, followed by his Eton chaplaincy and his directorship of the Education Leadership and Ministry program at Yale. In our time together after he left Roxbury Latin, he seemed interested in and reasonably well informed about developments at the school, but he never opined critically; about Kerry Brennan he had nothing but praise.

Tony's decision to depart gracefully is by no means typical. In fact, the inability of retiring headmasters of long and distinctive tenure to let go of the reins is an unresolved independent school problem. Whether or not they intend it, length-and-shadow headmasters pose problems for their successors. For colleagues and constituents who revere longstanding school heads, the successor may never seem good enough. There tends never to be another Peabody of Groton or Boyden of Deerfield. Boyden's case might stand as a cautionary example of what can happen when schools seem to be unimaginable without their headmaster.

Frank Boyden's astonishing sixty-six years on the job, in retrospect, may have been a few decades too long; the remarkable character he revealed for nearly a half century was reduced, in some colleagues' and students' experience, to caricature—as when in his last years at Deerfield Boyden was concerned that maybe some of the boys were smoking "maharaja."

Jack Pidgeon, one of several Deerfield faculty who would go on to head schools in the way Boyden modeled for them, led the Kiski School outside of Pittsburgh for forty-six years. Jack was a friend of mine and a beloved presence in his very distinctive school, but on his retirement, he chose to live on campus and to teach a favorite course. Understandably, he was the person alums would want to see when they returned to campus for games and reunions. There was, in effect, too little room for his successor to operate and for the school to move on. Sadly and reluctantly, the trustees had, in effect, to remove him from the campus.

In Tony's last weeks of life, he would tell Kerry Brennan what he had said to him many times since Kerry returned to lead Roxbury Latin: "KPB, you should know that the first thing I do upon waking each morning is to thank God that you are at the helm." Kerry felt the sentiment was genuine:

One could not have predicted, given Tony's uncompromising certitude how everything should be done, that he would be such a supportive, complimentary booster of his successor. I never had a doubt that Tony had my back and felt that whatever moves I made and utterances I offered, he would support me.

That support and Kerry's vision for the school would bear fruit. I am confident that if Tony were alive today he would agree that the school has never been better. By standard measures—selectivity, students' tested ability, admission to highly selected colleges—Roxbury Latin is impressive. In the dubious "ratings" industry that has arisen in the decades since *The U.S. News & World Report* began ranking American colleges and universities in 1983, Roxbury Latin is invariably rated as one of the leading private schools in the United States.

In addition to being a high performing school, Roxbury Latin is in some important ways a *different kind* of private school. Through the centuries since its colonial founding the school has made special provisions to admit the sons of poor families and for years designated the number of students who would attend for no cost. With an endowment of about 175 million dollars—$600,000 per pupil—the annual fees to attend are presently $15,000 to $20,000 less than those charged by other established day schools in the region. Moreover, whatever the stated cost of tuition, Roxbury Latin is one of the few schools in the country able to admit students "need blind." Boys are admitted for their personal and scholastic promise, without regard to their families' means. Once admitted, financial need is assessed and sufficient aid provided so that any boy admitted can attend. In consequence Roxbury Latin is eagerly sought by greater Boston families who believe they have a promising son but would not otherwise consider the expense of a private school.

While it is necessarily subjective to generalize about the character and feel of a school, merit-based, need-blind admission has resulted in an economically and otherwise diverse student body that has over the years seemed to be distinctly unentitled and un-"preppy." Because the school neither depends on nor caters to economically well-off families, and because it enrolls boys from any family geographically able to get them to West Roxbury every day, there is a prevailing absence of an in-crowd or an in-type. Given its intense scholastic and extra-curricular demands, Roxbury Latin tends to replace former neighborhoods and affiliations as the center of the boys' lives. The school is for every new boy a highly distinctive world, a world which Kerry Brennan at 22 found "comfortable for me and my kind," a school whose catalog still states its mission is to be a place where "every boy is known and loved."

Roxbury Latin today is a school Tony Jarvis restored and Kerry Brennan continues to revive. There are features of school life today that Tony would not have imagined. For example, the school now offers summer programs; Tony felt he needed to restore himself over the summer months and thus the campus must go quiet. Today students have the opportunity to study Spanish. There are new opportunities and spaces in which to build and design things, including robotics. There are new student seminars in leadership, new opportunities for student community service. There is now a splendid hockey facility and synthetic playing field surfaces. And because Kerry Brennan is Kerry Brennan, the entire school community gathers at holiday time for a joint singing of Handel's *Messiah.* Yet animating the school is the lively pulse of what has gone before.

On March 4th of every school year, the boys of Roxbury Latin have celebrated Exelauno Day, an eccentric state occasion created by a venerable Roxbury Latin classics master, Clarence William "Pop" Gleason, who taught Latin and Greek (and penmanship) between 1889 and 1939. Though he taught schoolboys for a half century, Gleason was the author of highly regarded classical language texts and translations and may have been the leading classicist of his era. He was especially expert on Xenophon's master work, *Anabasis*, a fourth century B.C.E. text recounting how a band of Greek mercenary soldiers made their grueling slog on foot from Persia back to Greek soil after a massive military defeat. Translating the text over the course of a school year was also something of a grueling slog for the Roxbury Latin boys, so Gleason determined to lighten the ordeal with a pun. Repeated through the *Anabasis* text is the Greek phrase *exelauno,* or "march forth." On March 4, 1934 Gleason put the boys in mind of the pun by declaring a moratorium on homework. What afterward became an Exelauno tradition at Roxbury Latin has spread to schools and colleges across the country.

The tradition was fondly remembered by Roxbury Latin graduates, and in 1957 an endowment was raised to subsidize Exelauno Day prizes for declamations in Latin and Greek presented by classics scholars in every grade. Tony loved Exelauno Day, as does Kerry Brennan who wrote of this year's festivities:

Boys representing each Latin and Greek section (17 this year) recite memorized passages from diverse classical texts. They perform with verve (and occasional histrionics) and, if appropriate, great poignancy. A trio of three distinguished judges determines the winners. Then the school gathers in Rousmaniere Hall and sings lustily several songs and hymns in Latin. It is one of our great state occasions. On Exelauno Day I will hear from alumni scattered all over the world. Some get together and raise a celebratory glass as they sing a round or two of Gaudeamus Igitur. They want to register that Exelauno Day is still seared in their memories.

LAST MEAL

———————

As we had arranged when he told me he had discontinued his chemotherapy and would let his mortal diagnosis run its course, I drove down to Boston by myself to have dinner with Tony. It had been more than a week since we last spoke on the phone, and I was prepared to find him in some kind of diminished condition. Not the case.

Tony greeted me at his door in high spirits. He was moving well and his color was good. We chatted cheerfully for an hour or so, mainly about his coming book, *Men of Roxbury*, brief lives of historic high achievers who attended Roxbury Latin School over the past three and a half centuries. I asked him about how his body felt, and as in our recent get-togethers, he expressed surprise at how comfortable he was. The inoperable tumors are in his lungs, and there are signs that the cancer has metastasized elsewhere including his brain, but he said there was no pain, no coughing, no shortness of breath. A month earlier his doctors told him he might expect eight "good" weeks. If he had any wistful feelings about not being alive when *Men of Roxbury* was published this coming year, I detected no trace.

Tony had made reservations at a restaurant he liked about a half mile from his flat, and he insisted that we walk. Over food and drinks we reminisced, gossiped, and kidded each other for nearly three hours. Tony managed to convey something like elation that the likely progression of his final weeks and days was at last clear. He has always been meticulous about managing his personal business, and his affairs, down to the last picture, asset, and personal file, were in order. I noticed that he lost our train of conversation several times. He said this was new and he hated it. Otherwise, he seemed cheerfully at ease. He told me that he had recently taken the train to New York to say farewell to longtime friends and while there realized he had had quite enough of New York. He said, "Honestly, I have done everything I wanted to do, gone everywhere I wanted to go."

My plan was to continue on to the Cape where I would join my wife who was doing babysitting duty for our daughter Jesse's children. Tony walked me back to my car, and we parted on an exuberant note, neither of us feeling a need to acknowledge out loud that this was most likely our last meeting. I drove off in an elevated state of mind, certain that even when Tony has gone atmospheric, he will be vividly present to me. At least consciously, I do not believe I have much dread of death, but driving south to the Cape that night I felt none at all.

Acknowledgements

M emory has been essential in this tribute to my friend, Tony Jarvis, but memories, however fond, are not always reliable. My efforts to avoid misremembering have been greatly aided by generous collaboration and review on the part of many people who have looked over this manuscript and have corroborated my account of Tony with their own experiences in his company. Chief among them are Tony's Roxbury Latin colleague and his successor as headmaster, Kerry Brennan, and Tony's assistant headmaster, Mike Pojman. Tony's longstanding friend Sally Muspratt and his brother-in-law Craig Smith shed needed light on Tony's university days at Harvard and Cambridge. Two of Tony's students at Yale Divinity School, Win Bassett and Tyler Montgomery, have been both generous and eloquent in sharing their impressions of Tony at work in his last teaching post. I am grateful for the care Tim Carey and Bob Ryan took to share their distinctive perspective on the challenges Tony faced on his arrival at The Roxbury Latin School. Carolyn Peter, the former head of the

Winsor School in Boston and Tony's long-time working colleague, deepened my appreciation of Tony's gift of friendship. Eton College housemaster Mike Grenier shared his impressions of Tony's post-retirement tour of duty there as an Eton College chaplain. My understanding of what may be the most unusually celebrated high school football victory in scholastic sports history was greatly enhanced by the details provided by then Roxbury Latin football coach and now Boston Trinity Academy headmaster Frank Guerra. Fr. Michael Godderz, Rector of All Saints, Ashmont, Tony's beloved Boston parish of more than forty years, and All Saints organist Andrew Sheranian contributed beautiful tributes to Tony's place in the parish. Jere Wells, who succeeded Tony as Director of the program for Educational Leadership and Ministry at the Yale Divinity School, shared appreciative insights on how Tony guided that extraordinary program into being.

Dozens of others, while not referenced in the text, have shared experiences and memories that have held my half-century regard for Tony firmly in place. To all of you memory fortifiers, I extend heartfelt gratitude. Together we may extend the luminous presence of this much beloved and remarkable man.

– R.A.H.

About the Author

R ichard Hawley is the former headmaster of University School in Cleveland and the founding president of the International Boys Schools Coalition. A writer of fiction, poetry, and literary non-fiction, he has published more than twenty books and  several monographs. His essays, articles and poems have appeared in dozens of literary, scholarly, and commercial journals, including *The New York Times*, *The Atlantic*, *American Film*, *Commonweal*, *America*, *Orion*, *The New England Journal of Medicine*, *The Christian Science Monitor*, and in a number of literary anthologies.

For ten years he taught fiction and non-fiction writing at the Bread Loaf Writers Conference in Vermont. Recent work, including work in progress, draws increasingly from depth psychology and classical philosophy to illuminate contemporary problems.